Insights
For
Young Mothers

Carol Rischer

HARVEST HOUSE PUBLISHERS
Eugene, Oregon 97402

INSIGHTS FOR YOUNG MOTHERS

Copyright © 1986 by Harvest House Publishers
Eugene, Oregon 97402

Library of Congress Catalog Card Number 85-081938
ISBN 0-89081-485-6

Printed in the United States of America.

Dedicated to
PAUL
my husband,
pastor, and
best friend.
And to our loving daughters
Melanie
Cheryl
Deanna
who have provided
INSIGHT into my MOTHERING
and encouragement as I
have written about our progress.

Acknowledgements

My first thank you goes to my mentors and dearest friends, Dan and Erna Jantz, who have shared their vision, their love, their encouragement, and their belief in what God is doing in my life. Their example of excellence in ministry motivates me daily.

I greatly appreciate the prayer support of many close friends and my family. An extra dose of thanks goes to my sister, Darlene Thomas, whose phone calls week after week and creative ideas nudged me on.

Thank you to my parents, Doug and Sue Corbett, for "training up a child in the way she should go" and for their warm Florida hospitality enabling me to complete my editing in solitude and sunshine.

Thank you to my typists: Debbie Gervais; Sue Fleurke; my sister-in-law, Joyce Rischer; my dear neighbor, Pam Lien; and especially Cheryl Leininger for her word processing skills.

Thank you to my number-one fan, lover, best friend, and motivator, Paul, without whose help and encouragement I could not have accomplished this labor of love.

Contents

Introduction

Recently my husband, Paul, and I were guests at a very special banquet. As a result we will never be the same.

It was the annual "Love Your Parents" dinner on Valentine's night at Grace Church in Edina. The room was decorated with red crepe paper and hearts. The red place mats were autographed with words of appreciation by the teenagers. The program was filled with skits and songs and a slide presentation, all built around a family theme.

The highlight of the evening was when several teens stood and publicly thanked their parents for the years of good memories and solid parenting. "Thank you for always being there when I needed you," said one girl. A high school senior boy said, "Thank you for discipline. I never thought I'd be able to say that!" Another one said, "I take it for granted that you know I love you. I want to tell you tonight that I do love you." My eyes were filled with tears as another teenager said, "Dad and Mom, I can truly see God's character in you." After those words of appreciation, the minister of youth stood and prayed, "I've got to believe, God, that You are smiling tonight!"

The program was nearly over when our oldest daughter, Melanie, turned to Paul and me and expressed her own thankfulness for the good memories she had of our parenting.

As we drove home that night, I couldn't help but think of the words in Proverbs 31:28—"Her children rise up and bless her." What mother doesn't desire such recognition after years of changing diapers and picking up toys and making sandwiches and driving the kids nearly everywhere?

But how had I arrived at this blessing? How can any mother achieve the goal of a full-grown and appreciative child? I thought of the message by David Busby, the minister to students at Grace Church. He had challenged us at the banquet with this principle in Galatians 6:7: "Whatever a man sows, this he will also reap." These, he said, were the facts of life:

> You will reap *what* you sow.
> You will reap *more* than you sow.
> You will reap *later* than you sow.

As mothers raising children, those words are both exciting and terrifying. I am excited that all my work will pay off and I will reap the positive character I've sown in the lives of my children. I am terrified because I have already seen my children mimic my negative input.

I realize that no mother is perfect, but God will hold us responsible for what we sow. And our family and friends and the rest of the world will eventually see what we have sown—if they haven't already! "The buck stops here" should be every parent's slogan in raising children. We are responsible.

With such an awesome responsibility, we could all use some help. And that's what this book is all about. It's not that I have all the answers; I don't. But I know God is the source of wisdom for parenting, and I have experience with my own three daughters. For several years I've also had the privilege of interacting with many other mothers through seminars, Bible studies, and a call-in radio program.

How does a normal mother living in an average

American home succeed in rearing a normal child? And what about the woman who's preparing to be a mother? Does she have to learn everything the hard way, by experience only? That's what this book is about—providing solid, practical advice on a wide range of areas. This is a handbook, a resource to pick up when you have a question. It's a tool to help you prepare for the future.

So where do we begin? By sowing good seed. Proverbs 23:7 tells us, "As [a man] thinks within himself, so he is." As mothers we can worry about the exceptions—the prodigal sons, the Cains, the rebels. But when we focus on the negatives, we sow negative seed. Let's put away our negative thoughts. Let's instead become responsible for:

1. Seeking God's direction and will for our children.
2. Praying that God will cause our seed to grow for His honor and glory.
3. Educating ourselves regarding the how-to's of mothering.
4. Disciplining ourselves to apply daily the principles we have learned.

The results won't be obvious immediately since we reap later than we sow. But we can accomplish the task God has set before us. So let's learn all we can to develop the talents God has so graciously given us. Let's "mother" to the very best of our ability before God. Let's be good stewards of the lives He has placed in our care. Then we can experience fulfillment and success in our most important role as mothers.

—Carol Rischer

1

Beginning

Paul and I sat sipping Pepsis at our kitchen table. Our first year of marriage was a dream come true. Were we "playing house" or was this reality? Many of our friends had struggled, fought, and limped through their first years of marriage.

Paul and I had dated each other exclusively for four years before we married. We knew each other well... our likes and our dislikes, our dreams and our fears, our abilities and our shortcomings. Now we were discussing a major change in our idyllic lifestyle.

Paul opened the discussion by asking, "When do you think we should start our family?"

"You've got to be kidding!" I said. "I love my teaching position. My career is just starting to take off."

"I know, but so many of our friends have kids. I feel left out. We're asked to babysit our friends' kids and your nephew—and it's kind of fun. The rest of the time we listen to them bragging about how great their kids are or we look at the latest pictures of their kids. I want my own."

"Paul, I hear what you're saying. Babies are cute. But I'm not ready. I still feel like a kid myself. And I love our carefree lifestyle. This is where it's at for now. Besides, with you in school we couldn't afford it if I quit working right now. We'd be stuck in an apartment the rest of our lives."

"Don't you get tired of waiting for things?" Paul said with a sigh. "Waiting to get married? Waiting to graduate? Waiting to buy a house? Waiting to have a baby? Don't you get tired of our precise schedules and perfectly packaged lives? What if you found out you were pregnant? What if it just happened?"

"We'd roll with the punches and make the best of the situation. But I'd rather plan if we can."

A couple of years later, according to plan, the day of delivery arrived. Paul phoned an old college buddy of his and announced, "George! Guess what? I'm finally a father!"

"You're kidding!" said George. "You really did it? I didn't realize you were that serious about your religious convictions!"

"Not a priest, George...a *father!*...a daddy!"

Marriage Versus Motherhood

Some Christian women argue that "au naturel" is the only way to live. They insist that in the beginning God blessed a couple with one child, no children, five children, nine children, 17 children...whenever and whatever. I do believe that God has a perfect plan for each person's life. Paul and I have always wanted God's best for our lives and our marriage. At our wedding we sang a duet titled "Each for the Other and Both for the Lord." We truly meant it. But experiencing that in reality is a day-by-day evaluation.

Understanding God's purpose for marriage helped us. Genesis 2:18-25 explains God's desire for companionship. He first created Adam to fellowship with God Himself. But He also wanted Adam to have a human companion—one who would experience this new life with him. When God created woman, He declared how very good she was for man. And the primary reason she was so good was that she was his companion—his best friend, apart from God.

Part B of God's "companionship" plan was the multiplication of this marvelous creation. God was going to produce multiple "companionship-packages" and fill the earth with "goodness." This was the beginning of the family. God has revealed to us in His Word that He created man and woman for two purposes: companionship and procreation. Companionship is an absolute. Procreation has some options . . . or at least possibilities.

Scripture is applicable to the culture of the day. Our culture is not one where parents arrange marriages when their children are young. Our culture is not one where young couples live communally with their parents and grandparents, who all work together as a clan to house and feed the offspring along with the camels and sheep. Our culture is not one that feels great responsibility to multiply and fill the earth. Our personal success and wealth is not assessed by the number of children we have. We all recognize the overpopulation in so many areas of the world, along with its terrible famines. We are created as beings with free choice. Our particular culture is a culture of free choice.

- *YOU* choose your mate.
- *YOU* choose where you will live.
- *YOU* choose how you will support yourself.
- *YOU* choose when you will produce children.
- *YOU* choose how many children you will produce.

You and I both know we don't have 100 percent control over our lives. Our almighty God predetermines our physical makeup, our strengths and abilities, our weaknesses and handicaps, our heritage and parents. But He still allows us many choices. And I believe in God's will for our lives. The best choices we can make are decided by studying God's Word, seeking His mind, spending time in prayer, allowing Him to focus our thinking, and choosing what we believe He wants for us. God is God. He will always have the final say. But just as He allowed Adam and Eve to make choices, so He allows us to make our own choices. He longs to give us His fatherly advice (direction and wisdom) for making good choices. But you and I do make the choices!

Choose to Build a Family on a Firm Foundation

What's the perfect age to get married? What's the perfect age to have your first baby? How far apart should the children be spaced?

Most of us dream more realistically in retrospect. Each of us has secret insights into certain areas of motherhood that would be helpful to someone else if we got together and pooled our ideas and shared our discoveries. I'm sure we would all agree on one thing—the importance of a honeymoon period. When we get married, we want to celebrate our union and have time to get to know each other as husband and wife without the demands of parenting.

A few carefree years of focusing only on each other can build a strong foundation on which to build a family. Many couples use these years to travel, reasoning that if they don't get to Hawaii or Europe now, they won't get there for another 15 or 20 years. This kind of thinking is supported by women who have been married 20 years and are still trying to go to Hawaii. Many others use these years to complete the major portion of their education and thereby lay a foundation for financial security. Others cautiously save to reach their goal of purchasing their dream home.

Whatever your goals, use some time to build a solid foundation in your marriage relationship. Our society pulls us in so many directions, often tearing apart our marriages in the process. Newlyweds in the Old Testament were instructed by God to focus on their marriage alone for one full year. What a honeymoon! Deuteronomy 24:5 says, "When a man takes a new wife, he shall not go out with the army, nor be charged with any duty; he shall be free at home one year and shall give happiness to his wife whom he has taken."

Since our society does not afford such a luxury, I believe we need to apply the same principle and focus on our marriage relationship as much as possible when we first marry. We should work or study or achieve whatever primary goal we have agreed upon, and otherwise focus on each other. We should be as uninvolved as possible in extra activities and even extra ministries during our first year of marriage.

With regret I think of a gorgeous young couple who got married in our church in California. He was handsome, a beautiful singer and guitar player, a dedicated Christian who desired to enter the ministry. She was a beautiful girl with long, flowing blonde hair and a gorgeous figure, and was very intelligent. They were picture perfect . . . until they divorced a year later. The reason? He was totally consumed with his goals— his study, his prayer life, his ministry. She wanted to have some fun, but her Prince Charming had turned into a tyrant. His queen seemed frivolous and unmotivated. Even after much counsel, they would not focus on meeting each other's needs and providing the biblically mandated companionship. That's the balance we need to find. "Balance" is a word that we will evaluate and apply often as we discuss motherhood. Balance is certainly needed at the beginning of a marriage relationship.

Paul and I had a ball during our first few years of marriage. We would both come home from work or school on a Friday evening and decide what we wanted to do. Within 15 minutes we could throw some clothes in a suitcase, meet our good friends Warren and Heather, and head out of town for the weekend. We weren't responsible for anyone or to anyone. We celebrated our marriage relationship by spending a lot of time enjoying each other and relaxing with other newlyweds. We have many good memories of those years.

During those years we dreamed, we planned, we imagined what our children would look like, and we discussed values. As a couple we knew we should be unified in thought on areas such as whether I as a mother should stay home once the baby arrived, and, if so, whether this should be a temporary or permanent arrangement. We discussed who would be responsible for each of the household chores. (If these responsibilities are not shared when both mates are working, it is doubtful that it will happen when the wife is at home. The couple who shares responsibilities in household management before children arrive are the ones who will most likely share them after children arrive.)

We discussed our goals and dreams as a couple and as individuals. We affirmed each other, discussing different options and possibilities that might open doors for us to climb the mountains and reach for the stars. Perhaps our dreams would have seemed insignificant to another couple, but they weren't intended for another couple; they were for *us*. They represented our values. They represented who we are. They represented our life together.

This is the only life on earth you have, so dare to dream. Communicate openly with your spouse. If you need help, find someone who will help you. Don't be too timid or too embarrassed to tackle a communication problem that might erode the foundation of your marriage. You need to value your marriage very highly. You need to value and respect each other as individuals and as husband and wife. Use this time to establish yourselves securely as husband and wife, *before* you take on the additional roles of father and mother.

How do you know when you're ready to have a baby? A good question to ask is, "Who wants this baby the most?" If the answer is truly both of you, your chances of success in parenting are very high. If the answer is only one of you, don't make the mistake of trying to glue a marriage together by having a baby. A baby is not glue. A baby is exhaustion. A baby is a 24-hour-a-day, 365-day-a-year, 18-year responsibility! A baby is work. A baby is expense. A baby is an assignment harder than you ever faced in school. That's the bad news. The good news is that a baby brings joy one hundredfold in comparison to the work he demands. A baby is the most wonderful gift you will ever receive. By planning carefully, you will be able to invest yourself in this child and enjoy the blessings of your investment.

The fact that a baby will not hold a weak marriage together was tragically demonstrated by one of Paul's relatives. Keith was rebelling against responsibility and God's authority while his young Christian wife, Rhonda, dreamed of having a nice Christian home and becoming a mother. When she found herself pregnant, she hoped the baby would bring stability, fulfillment, and purpose to her husband and their marriage. But he saw the baby as a threat and he left, looking for greener pastures. She had to endure the pregnancy alone, deliver the baby alone, and cope as a single parent with exhausting days and tear-filled late-night feedings.

Fortunately this story has a happy ending. After months of prayer, God performed a miracle: Before the baby's first birthday, Keith rededicated His life to the Lord, asked Rhonda for forgiveness, and asked her to marry him again. My husband, who counseled them after their divorce, had the privilege of remarrying them, and this time they began to build a foundation for their marriage relationship with a security that was lacking before.

Unfortunately many children get thrown into the boxing ring of a bad marriage. Don't be pressured into having a child to try to glue your marriage together or for any other inappropriate reason. Don't be pressured into having a child because your parents are dying to be grandparents! Don't be pressured into having a child because your friends all have children and that's all they ever talk about and you feel left out. Don't be pressured into having a child because your friends aren't free to go out with you anymore because they can't get a babysitter, so you might as well be tied down yourself (since you feel tied down by their kids). Be confident enough to live according to God's timetable for *you*. Secure your marriage before you conceive your family. If your marriage foundation is wobbly, seek solid counseling. Construct a firm foundation for the future of your family.

Choosing When to Have a Child

I watched Cathy as she chased after her three little

ones, quieted them down, and set them up to play in the family room. We proceeded to take our afternoon tea into the living room. We were no sooner seated than little Jamie came in and attempted to crawl up on Mommy's knee. Meanwhile Jessie was swinging the guinea pig while Cathy called out, "Jess—be careful! And please don't sing so loud. Carol and I are trying to have a cup of tea together."

"Busy years, aren't these, Cathy?" I observed. "Not too many quiet moments. I know how difficult it is to carve out time for friends and time for husband and time for yourself."

She agreed. The years spent nursing babies and chasing toddlers *are* consuming. Our choice of when to go through this stressful period in our life is a luxury. Cathy and her husband purposefully waited to have their children until he had completed his medical degree and internship and she had finished her masters degree in business administration. They used their early years of marriage to establish their careers, and now they've set aside the necessary years to rear a family.

Jeahne, on the other hand, had her first child after 11 months of marriage and her second a couple of years later. She is not much older than Cathy, but her youngest will head for college this fall, leaving Jeannie and her husband free. She's enjoying trips to Hawaii and studying computers for her own personal fulfillment and to assist her husband in his business. She's still young and the world is waiting for her.

Motherhood: It's a lifelong privilege with a 20-to-30-year term in office! Twenty to 30 years sounds like a lifetime, but it really isn't. All of us younger mothers have had older women remind us, "Enjoy your children while they're young. These are the best years of your life. " We think, "You've got to be kidding! There must be no hope for the future!" But there is.

In setting aside five to ten years to take care of the "underfoot" years, you can choose *now* or *later*. You can work or study through your twenties and be tied down when other mothers are just beginning to be free (children off to school), or you can have your children while you're young so that when they're older you'll still be young enough to pick up a career or study a new profession or develop your creativity in whatever way you desire. You can have *your* time before, or after, or a little of both. The choice is up to you. (Of course I am not focusing here on women who cannot physically plan their pregnancies or because of special problems do not have the options that are available to other women. We'll discuss this a little later.)

Firm Foundations and Finances

John is planning to save enough money to pay cash for a home. *Then* he plans to get married and have a family. John is handsome, intelligent, and a dedicated Christian. He dates only casually because he says he isn't ready for marriage yet. I have known John 13 years, and I'll eat my hat the day John reaches his goal. It's unrealistic.

In contrast, Howard says the Lord is going to return any day, so there's no need to plan for the future. He refuses to "get caught up with" settling into a house, rearing a family, and becoming consumed with "material things."

Balance? There's that word again.

The majority of couples I know do plan. We are taught to set financial goals and make specific plans as to how these goals can be realized. If you want a home, as most couples do, two incomes are often necessary for a few years to save for a down payment. The key is to live solely on one income and save the other. After you find your house, continue to live on one income as much as possible so that after your baby is born you will be able to live on your husband's income alone (when you won't have yours to fall back on). Of course, this system won't work if your husband is still in school. Your finances might have to be used out of necessity in order to lay an educational foundation rather than a concrete foundation.

Although it is wise to map out financial goals and achieve some of these before you start a family, there is a danger in letting your desire for more education or more material things take over. Many couples miss out on the greatest blessings of life because their realistic goals slowly become selfish, unachievable wants.

So prayerfully consider God's priorities and timetable for your family.

Consider Your Age

Sue was around 30 when she married, and she had three children in the following six years. Before marriage Sue had an exciting career of travel and ministry. Her husband was an established lawyer, so there was no need to frantically save for a house. They had enjoyed the benefits of single life in their twenties. Now they were ready to settle down.

If you marry in your late twenties or early thirties, you may not have the luxury of waiting years before starting a family. Medical journals tell us our bodies are better able to conceive and deliver healthy babies at younger ages. If you are beginning a family in your thirties, you should consider the care of your body in determining how many children to have and how to space them. By marrying later, you have probably brought more maturity into your marriage and, though the prechild days are important, they may not be as crucial for you. You have already had many care-free years and experienced more of life as an independent adult.

Timing Techniques

For the sake of example, let's get married at age 22 after graduating from college and starting a career. Of course we marry Prince Charming, knowing that he's all we've ever dreamed of and is definitely God's choice. Let's enjoy four or five years of wedded bliss. At age 26 or 27 let's have our first child. Let's have a second around age 29 or 30, and maybe even a third around age 32 or 33.

How are you feeling? Your reaction may help you determine what you believe is a better plan for you at your particular age and in your particular circumstances.

My children are not three years apart, but in retrospect that would have been much easier spacing. Children a year or two apart often experience intense competition, especially as they get older. My sister, Jan, and I were 18 months apart. Growing up was a struggle because she was nearly as old as I was and nearly able to do all that I could do (and able to do many things much better than I could).

I now have two daughters 19 months apart, and I observe the same tendencies in them. The younger one struggles to grow up as fast as the older one. The older one struggles to maintain her own identity at her "older" age. Neither has to prove anything, yet each thinks she does. They are both in junior high school and have both begun to babysit. The opportunities arose, and both girls are capable. Yet Cheryl will be doing it at a year-and-a-half younger than Melanie. This doesn't seem fair to Melanie. Well, life isn't fair. On many issues we have remained strict about having a certain privilege at a certain age. That has helped, but areas of friction like this can harm a relationship between siblings. If I could avoid it, I would.

Children three or so years old are usually toilet-trained, which means that if a new baby arrives, you have only one child in diapers at a time. A three-year-old understands "no" and can understand verbal directions. It's a much easier age for mothers! Yet children three or so years apart are still close enough in age to enjoy playing together and growing up together and experiencing family vacations together. Children six to ten years apart find it more difficult to relate and maintain any closeness.

How Many Children?

In determining how many children you plan to have, you may have a blueprint number, but you need to reassess this number *after each child is born*. After you evaluate, decide if or when to expand.

Consider first of all your *health*. As a mother you need to consider your health above all. You have brought a new life into this world, and you need to properly care for this child. Don't be a martyr and give your family second best. Heed the medical warnings if your doctors are concerned with your safety and health.

Consider next your *social well-being*. As a mother your total health involves your emotional well-being and social relationships. You need to function as a whole person, so be aware of your personal needs.

Don't give your all to having babies because then you will have nothing left to raise them. Your husband wants a happy wife. He does not want an existence with an exhausted woman near collapse at the end of each day due to her daily chores and many children.

Consider your *living conditions*. Do you have adequate space to house another human being? I am not suggesting an exaggerated standard of living, but I am suggesting *planning* what you will be able to provide for your child. Adequate living space is important to a cultured family life.

Consider your *financial security*. Does your husband's employment look secure? No person knows the future, and God alone is our provider, but He expects us to plan and to work! Before I married, my father reviewed with Paul the responsibilities he was undertaking. Dad discussed with Paul the Scripture, "If anyone does not provide for his own . . . he . . . is worse than an unbeliever" (1 Timothy 5:8). Dad reaffirmed his love for us, stating that he and Mom would always be there to love and support and pray for us—which they have. And in time of need we could come to them and they would help us if they could. But the *responsibility* of providing for our family lay squarely on Paul's shoulders.

So . . . how many children should a couple have? Only *you* can properly evaluate this critical decision. With God's direction, plan what you believe is best. In America we are not influenced as much by "population explosion" problems as are some other countries of our world. I believe you need to sit down as a couple and decide how many children you dream of and think you can properly rear. Children should not be conceived without considering the training and education that needs to follow. No child asks to be born. They don't owe us; we owe them an upbringing...training...discipline...time...and love.

Responsible parenting does not necessarily mean having only a few children. Responsible parenting means evaluating and planning and praying and rearing children as a glory to the Lord.

"Whatever you do, do all to the glory of God" (1 Corinthians 10:31).

Too Late to Plan

If you have read this far, you may be thinking, "Planning must be nice, but you're too late for me." Maybe you already have six children—the first one born before you were married. Maybe you feel your household is out of control. Or your children are disobedient. Or your husband is preoccupied and too tired to care. You're discouraged and exhausted just trying to hold things together.

You do need some positives in your life. Yes, these difficult days will pass, but I would love to help you face these days with a plan that will help you survive and succeed! Accept this *promise* and this *challenge* from God:

> PROMISE: "We know that God causes all things to work together for good to those who love God, to those who are called according to His purpose" (Romans 8:28).

> CHALLENGE: "One thing I do: Forgetting what lies behind and reaching forward to what lies ahead" (Philippians 3:13).

Day by day, area by area, page by page, chapter by chapter, let God turn your despair and exhaustion into fulfillment and success. Let's work through the process together.

2

The Joys of Birth and Nursing

Pregnancy

Paul sat beside me on the floor. I sat cross-legged on the pillow I'd brought from home and counted slowly as I exercised "pant, blow, pant, blow." Most of the couples in the room were anticipating the arrival of their first babies. One couple was expecting their second. We were expecting our third. In our Prepared Childbirth classes they called us the "Old Pros," but as experienced as we were, I was still apprehensive. Each birth is so different. I knew it would help to mentally prepare myself and practice those relaxation breathing exercises with a good support group. A few husbands laughed and teased us about our breathing techniques, but *they* weren't the ones delivering the babies!

Not every woman had a supportive husband. A single mother sat next to me with a friend who had offered to be her coach. My husband encouraged her as she prepared to deliver this baby. She had fears, as does every woman who faces childbirth. Much fear can be alleviated through proper knowledge and understanding—and that's why we were all at this class together.

We had all passed the halfway point of our pregnancies. Many had come through three or more months of throwing up each morning, sleeping each afternoon, and craving pickles, pizza, or pralines and cream each evening. Being fat was new to some and old hat to others who had struggled with weight most of their lives. Being pregnant was a dream for some, a miracle for others (who had tried every type of medical assistance available and had finally conceived), and a disaster for another, who had just been jilted by her boyfriend. My heart went out to all of them.

There are some women who find themselves pregnant but they don't want to be, or they have no husband. This is a time to rely totally on God. No, you would not have chosen this, but you cannot continually condemn yourself or constantly rehearse the injustice of your situation. You can choose to apply Romans 8:28 and let God work this for good. Take good care of yourself during this time of pregnancy— whether you plan to keep the baby or place it for adoption by a family who has prayed for such a blessing. There will be negative people, perhaps some close family members, who are more concerned about their reputation than your well-being. So try to spend quality time with a few positive supporters. Every pregnant woman, and you especially, needs encouragement, support, and an extra measure of tender loving care.

For those women who are happily married, months of pregnancy are a special opportunity to develop a tender bond with their mates. Even in this equal-rights era, with capable women maintaining careers and doing aerobic exercises till the day they deliver, this is too precious a time not to share with your lover—letting him care for you in a special way, flexing his protective muscles in preparation for his own parenthood. If your husband is willing, pray together for your unborn child and your future as a parent. You might also read a few Bible verses together and meditate on God's guidelines for your lives.

I realize that not all husbands feel comfortable praying with their wives. Nancy dropped by for coffee one morning. When I asked her how things were going, she didn't give me the standard "Fine, great, really good, thanks." She shared that for years she felt like she had missed that extra-special closeness in her marriage relationship because her husband would not pray with her. Her husband was a Christian but excused himself because this was too personal an area for him to share. I assured Nancy that she wasn't the only woman who felt so deprived. In fact many pastors' wives have confessed the same problem to me. Some men have a difficult time sharing intimately on any emotional level, and their relationship with God represents their deepest emotional level. Many other men feel belittled by their spiritual-giant wives who live at Bible studies and memorize every impressive phrase that might be used in prayer to show their "spirituality." We need to remember that a man's spiritual walk should not be measured by his verbal skills.

If your husband will pray with you, I believe you can share a new tenderness together. This may be the first time in your lives when you feel totally helpless as you contemplate new responsibilities and changes in your lifestyle. God can use this tender time to build bridges and unite you spiritually.

The basics of a healthy pregnancy should be common knowledge. As in everyday life, now especially we are to eat nutritiously, exercise moderately, sleep adequately, and pray excessively! We need to conscientiously keep our doctor appointments and follow his advice. We should continue to pay attention to personal grooming—dressing attractively, reflecting a positive attitude, using cosmetics to enhance our radiance, and enjoying our femininity at its peak. I highly recommend Prepared Childbirth classes or Lamaze courses as the best way to prepare physically and psychologically for childbirth. If possible, take a class with your husband.

Finally, enjoy the silly moments that will arise before your baby is born. Paul and I climbed into bed early one evening shortly before our first child was born. "Don't you crave anything?" he asked. I took the bait: "Why? Are you hungry?" "Right on. I thought you might be craving a pizza again, and I want to take care of your needs." I laughed as he walked to the telephone. If our budget could afford it, why not let both of us crave?

Waiting for the pizza to arrive, Paul rested his hands on my tummy and felt the baby kick and jab. A few days earlier Paul had gone with me to the doctor and heard his baby's heartbeat. Yes, "we" were truly pregnant!

Childbirth

Jan lay on the delivery table, bearing down with another hard contraction. Terry waited outside, wanting to be supportive but knowing his limitations at a time like this. Fathers were not allowed in delivery rooms in those days, so he paced and prayed in the father's room as the minutes seemed like hours. Suddenly he froze as he heard his wife scream in the midst of a particularly intense contraction. Then as the pain subsided he heard Jan yell, "That darn Eve!"

Whether alone or with your mate or a supportive friend, you will experience what Jan did when she delivered her baby—helplessness and the awareness of the presence of God. Genesis 3:16 states, "In pain you shall bring forth children."

Prepared Childbirth classes teach us to never focus on the negative word "pain." Through their education and films showing live births they eliminate 90 percent of our fears, which eliminates a great deal of unnecessary pain. Still, the pain of some very hard work awaits most deliveries. Being prepared as husband and wife for what might take place is the way to go these days.

Because of this new openness and available education, many husbands are prepared to participate in the miracle of the birthing process. Paul was one of the first fathers I knew who went with his wife to the delivery room. Melanie was born in early 1972, and he was excited about our "project." When the time for Melanie's delivery arrived, Paul was scrubbed and by my side. Between contractions and moans and groans, I propped myself up on my elbows and watched my baby's birth by peering in the overhead mirror. Paul reached for our wet, screaming newborn and set her on my stomach. Then the doctor let Paul cut the umbilical cord. Knowing that this privilege is not available to all couples, I hesitate to rave about this obvious highlight in our lives. But for those who have the opportunity to experience this immediate bonding of father to daughter, mother to daughter, and father to mother in their new role as parents, I highly recommend it. The tenderness of those memories we shared continue to bind our closeness.

No matter how many babies we have, every birth is unique. With Melanie I suffered from toxemia and spent the last three weeks of my pregnancy in the hospital. For our second baby I remained healthy the whole way. Cheryl was born on a Sunday evening. I played the piano for our church service, then sauntered across the parking lot. As I got into our car, my water broke! Paul frantically drove me home, called the doctor, called a friend to take care of our toddler, then drove to the hospital. Within 45 minutes Cheryl was born and within 34 hours I was back home—now a mother of two infants in diapers.

We waited 4½ years before we had our third baby. This time I was three weeks overdue and pleaded with my physician to induce labor. He finally agreed and I delivered a ten-pound, two-ounce star! Within 22 hours I was back home again. Paul's involvement in the birthing and bonding again provided a special memory.

Each couple's experiences are unique. Each couple's dreams differ. Each couple's opinions determine their plans and practices. The controversy over birthing procedures and practices varies from location to location and family to family. Here are some options you may consider.

Hospital or Home?

Pauline delivered her baby at home because she didn't want to go into debt over her medical bills. The baby was going to cost enough without delivery room expenses and hospital care billed by the hour.

June delivered her latest baby at a birthing center where her older children were allowed to be present. Later our family watched home movies of the event.

Jean delivered in the hospital. She had no desire to share such an intimate and personal experience. Her husband, Bob, felt the older children would be afraid their mother was going to die, even though that is extremely rare.

Partly because of exorbitant hospital costs and partly

because of the desire for intimacy and privacy, many modern couples opt for delivering their babies at home. However, you should consider what quality of medical help would be available should an emergency arise. I loved the home atmosphere of the "birthing rooms" in the hospital. The cheery wallpaper and homelike bedroom feel helped to relax me. But in my case I was wise to deliver in a hospital. My toxemia was properly treated in my first pregnancy, preventing poison from being fed to my fetus. My overdue baby needed oxygen immediately after she was born. (Postdue babies are as problem-prone as premature babies.)

In weighing out cost and convenience, consider first and foremost the health and safety of you and your baby.

And what about pictures? Jerry, a photographer friend of ours, was hired by a couple—not to do their wedding but to do the birth of their baby! He was on call and did in fact do the honors. You've heard of nervous fathers. He said he was a nervous photographer. I was content with Paul's amateur photography to preserve a few memories for the two of us. (No, you can't see my pictures!)

Natural Versus C-section Versus Adoption

Following an aerobics class, several women started talking in the locker room about their deliveries. One woman proudly announced, "I delivered my baby naturally. What an exhilarating experience—the only way to go! Any mother who really cares about the welfare of her baby will refuse drugs or any artificial help offered her."

Karen changed quietly in the corner. She couldn't bear to have a second baby if she couldn't ask for some type of medication to ease the pain. It hadn't harmed her first baby. But she didn't dare speak up and let these other gals think she was such a chicken. Linda also remained quiet. She had had a C-section. She now felt left out as these women raved about the wonders of natural childbirth.

Linda and Karen don't need to feel ashamed. No one procedure is more honorable than another. You owe no one an explanation for your birthing procedure. Your focus and purpose is to take the best possible care of you and your baby. True, you will want to use as few drugs as possible to protect the health of your baby and to remain as alert as possible so you won't miss this very special experience. The more you read and study about giving birth, the more you will relax and be able to make wise decisions and experience the richness of these areas of mothering.

Adoption is another "birthing procedure," and in many instances it's the most difficult method of delivering a baby.

John and Debbie made three gallant attempts to adopt. Debbie is committed to full-time mothering and John is a lawyer who is financially secure. One baby was denied them because the baby's grandparents, full of hatred and bitterness over their child's immorality, decided to keep the child and "cope" with this disgraceful product of their past. Another baby was denied them because the state ruled against Caucasians adopting biracial babies. The third attempt found their name sitting dormant on a waiting list for two years. Two questions affect their future: Will their emotions allow them to continue their pursuit? And will their age stop them? Biological age is not crucial for adoptive parents, and many couples are choosing to add to their families later in life. They can afford the time and the money and look forward to this rewarding experience. Yet many states set ages of 37 to 40 as the cutoff for adoptive mothers.

While John and Debbie wait, Jim and Sharon share a success story. Once the adoption was legally agreed upon, they met the natural mother and each party assured the other of their number one interest—the welfare of the child. This unwed mother had had two abortions prior to delivering this baby. She now acknowledged that innocent children should not pay the price for their parents' irresponsibility. Innocent children should not be labeled illegitimate; the label belongs to the parents. Innocent children, prayed for by hopeful adoptive parents, should not be aborted.

Adoption is a process that often takes many years and costs thousands of dollars. But it's worth it. In fact, an adoptive baby is a double blessing: God has provided a family for a child who needs a home, and God has provided a baby for a mother who needs a family.

Nursing: Bottle or Breast?

Now that the baby is born, we are ready for one of the most enjoyable periods of motherhood. However, there are moments when we might wonder. One Sunday morning I sat at the piano at church ready to play a congregational hymn following my offertory solo. Wayne, a good friend a number of years older than I, walked down with the choir and whispered as he passed, "Must be time to go and nurse your baby." I looked down at my dress and discovered two huge wet circles on my blouse. The joys of motherhood? I wanted to crawl under the piano bench.

In spite of occasional inconveniences and awkward situations, I'm an enthusiastic believer in breast-feeding! God created our breasts to nourish our newborns. However, like childbirth, breast-feeding is an area where there is so much they never tell you. I knew the advantages of nursing..."natural" milk with no preservatives added. I knew the blessing of nursing....continuing the bonding process. But no one ever told me that nursing hurts! We're talking pain! Women talk about the *joy* of nursing. True—like the *joy* of giving birth. There is work and pain involved for the first few days or weeks.

The pain of uterine contractions while the milk is beginning to flow, the pain of tender breasts while the milk engorges and finally regulates its production level, the pain of sore nipples while the skin "toughens up," the pain of depression following weaning—it's truly worth it compared to the joy experienced through the bonding and intimacy of nursing. After the first few weeks of nursing, the joy to me ranks second only to the intimacy of intercourse with my mate. Life offers very few such intimate, pure, and rewarding relationships. So if at all possible, don't miss out on another of God's private gifts to you as a mother.

True, not all women can nurse. If nursing is a physical impossibility for you, do not dwell on this negative, but focus on all the positives in your life! Feeding your baby should be one of the most relaxing times of your day. Don't rush. And if you're not breast-feeding, give your baby the bottle yourself. You deserve the quiet time when the baby is usually happiest and you can relax.

If nursing is something you've considered but decided to abandon because of negative input you've received, don't cheat yourself! Don't assume you could never learn to swim because there's a possibility you could drown. As in 90 percent of the tasks you undertake in life, it's mind over matter.

There are inconveniences: You might feel tied to your baby at first. During her pregnancy Jo Ann read the manuals which said that babies nurse every four hours. She thought this sounded reasonable until her son was born and was starved every hour-and-a-half! Many women relate stories of being bitten by a four-month-old who mysteriously grew his first tooth one night while sleeping and attacked his mother first thing in the morning.

A secondary inconvenience is having to wear a nursing bra. I don't mind it during the day, but all the time? For first-time moms, let me mention here that there are now beautiful nursing fashions available at most maternity shops. Pretty nightgowns are made with convenient slits in the folds of fabric which make nursing very simple at night.

Nursing is more than a physical experience; it is also a mental exercise: You must believe you can do it. Don't let people disturb you by asking, "Are you sure the baby's getting enough milk? He cries so much. Don't you think a supplement would help?" I think encouragement and positive input would help! Negative people can cause doubts that affect your performance in many areas of life. Nursing is one of those fragile areas. If certain friends or relatives are down on nursing, it might be important for your own sake to spend less time with them during this period and spend more time with positive, enthusiastic encouragers.

I remember one bubbly lady at our church who must have had the gift of encouragement. Marge would hug me and say, "Isn't motherhood wonderful! I know you're nursing. Cherish every minute of it. Any discomfort is worth it. You are such a special mother and you have the most precious baby!" Of course I believed her!

Sometimes your doubting Thomas is a family member who will come to spend time with the baby. You feel nervous at the thought. Even this nervousness can affect your nursing ability. While you must be polite, you must also believe that you and your baby are most important. Even if you are normally a "Martha," even if you are usually the one to sacrifice so grandparents or friends can enjoy their visit, don't do it at this time. Allow others to minister to you for awhile. Is no one picking up your workload? Then let chores slide for awhile.

Negative input can actually inhibit your breast flow. One afternoon I was happily and confidently nursing my infant when a close family member who was visiting walked into the room and remarked, "I sure hope that little one's getting the nourishment she needs. All that crying last night—she'd sleep longer if she had more in her tummy." Consciously I thought I was handling those remarks just fine. Subconsciously I was not. My milk actually stopped flowing! The baby started to fuss and cry. I became embarrassed. My negative-thinking person had her proof—verification that she was right.

When you run into "N.T.'s" (negative thinkers), say "N.T." in your mind (no thanks!).

Without verbalizing my "N.T.," I quietly excused myself and retreated to the bedroom. With the door closed and no distractions, I relaxed. My milk began to flow and my baby began to nurse again. Part of loving your baby is loving yourself. Be secure enough to take good care of the two of you. Say "No Thanks" to "Negative Thinkers," even if it's only in your mind.

It would be helpful for you to read books on nursing—especially *The Womanly Art of Breast-feeding*, prefaced by La Leche League International. It will help you understand the production of milk in relationship to the sucking you allow your infant, and also the day-or-so delay between demand and supply. Baby will have some fussy days, but overall you'll feel satisfied in transferring your immunities to your infant, warding off colds and infectious diseases, and providing the best nutrition possible.

Nursing: Manners and Modesty

My mom was serving coffee to her neighborhood ladies. One of them, Joy, sat nursing her infant when into the room ran her two-year-old son. Older women watched in amazement as this big lug of a boy climbed up onto Joy and started sucking on her other breast. Those neighbors had lots to talk about the rest of that day.

I am not a purist La Leche League nursing mother. When my babies could run up and ask for a drink, I gave them a cup! I nursed my babies about ten months each—six months before I supplemented at all. As they grew a full set of teeth I weaned them to eat solid food—not me!

Weaning can be an emotional time for mother as well as baby. Any abrupt weaning can be painful, sometimes requiring the breasts to be bound. Gradual weaning is easier but can still leave Mom feeling kind of depressed for a month or so. That's understandable when you realize all the changes your body has gone through in the last year or longer. You've experienced emotional ups and downs as your hormones have trampolined within you. So relax and be a little easy on yourself. Realize that many other nursing mothers have weaned their babies and experienced the same thing. A call to your local La Leche League might provide the support you need from someone who has been there and can assure you that time will restore your emotional balance.

Now a final word about nursing manners. I prefer to nurse alone, although I am quite relaxed with a close friend over a cup of coffee. I prefer to nurse at home, but I have done my share of nursing in restaurants, parks, church nurseries, or friends' homes—wherever the need arose. But I hope I have remembered the Golden Rule and not embarrassed anyone. We need to be discreet, use good manners, and maintain modesty. We have to remind ourselves to be modest at this time in our lives because we have just been exposed to the world—or so it seems—losing all privacy as we bore our children. Now that our world revolves around changing diapers and breast pads and getting postnatal medical checkups, our private life seems a thing of the past.

Feminism and gracious manners are a gift to yourself and to others. A blouse that lifts up is more discreet than a top or dress you must unbutton from the neck down. A lightweight blanket draped over the baby can completely cover the exposed nipple and breast area.

In your attempt to be well-mannered, still be your natural self. If a youngster runs up to you to see your baby drinking milk, don't be embarrassed. Your wholesome attitude is the education we desire for our children. You are a perfect picture of motherhood.

Nursing is one duty of motherhood—work, but really quite enjoyable. Whether you choose to nurse or bottle-feed, the loving care you give your child and these tender moments between the two of you are what really count. Enjoy this beauty now and enjoy the memories you will have for life.

3

Diaper Days and
Other Tedious Tasks

"What's that awful smell?"

As I recall diaper days, I think of Murphy's Law, and its corollary, the Law of Selective Gravity. If anything can go wrong, it will. Diapering is never as easy as it looks. Changing a diaper will always take longer than you think. If you have to change a diaper while at a formal occasion, it will never be just a wet one—it will always be messy.

Life is not perfect when you have a diapered member in your family. Bill Butterworth, a favorite Southern California speaker of mine, suggests that we contrast idealism with realism and make our goal as parents *realistic success*. (If you have a child in diapers, you deserve to treat yourself to Bill's book *Peanut Butter Families Stick Together*.) Realistic success helps us to live the best life we can without worrying about what's beyond our control. *Having to change diapers* is beyond our control. *How we go about changing diapers* is an area where we can be realistically successful. Gracious manners and proper etiquette is a kindness you extend to others and to yourself. One of my pet peeves is having to be a part of another mother's diapering mess and/or horror stories. Control your urge to announce what you are about to tackle

41

or describe what you have just faced. Good manners means being discreet.

Before changing a diaper, gather the following supplies:

- Plastic-lined pad for under the baby (when away from home)
- Clean diaper
- Kleenex
- Wet cloth if sink is within reach, or wet disposable towelettes
- Powder and/or ointment
- Clean plastic pants
- Clean outer clothing for baby, if needed
- Plastic bag to house soiled diapers
- Second plastic bag to house soiled clothing
- Toy or rattle to keep baby occupied while you change his diaper

If you are at home, these supplies should be handy in your nursery. Keep everything within easy reach of the changing table. Keep the checklist by your diaper case so you're sure everything is packed when you go out. With all the supplies at your fingertips, you will not need to call out for help when you're in the middle of the change, and you will not have to leave the baby while you run to get something.

Never leave the baby while you're in the middle of a diaper change—not even to answer the phone. Safety first.

A private place is a must for diapering a child. Next to using a proper change-table in the baby's nursery, the best place is a bathroom. I find it safest to lay the child on the bath mat on the floor so I don't have to worry about him rolling off a counter. By diapering in the bathroom, all facilities are available should your child end up needing a bath! Also, you confine any smell to the proper room of the house.

If a bathroom is not available and you choose to diaper in a bedroom, *always* place a pad under the child's bottom and do not leave the child alone—not even for a minute. If you do not have a plastic-lined pad to lay under the child's bottom, borrow a towel.

I stress this because of Marion's experience. She loves to entertain. Her own children are grown, but she enjoys other people's children as she shares her home with many young couples from her church. Linda was over with her baby, and without asking went into the master bedroom to change her infant's diaper. Marion walked into her bedroom too late. Stains and wet spots revealed that baby had made a surprise attack on her 200-dollar bedspread. Linda was trying to sponge up the accident. I'm sure Linda realized that this was hardly the way to get asked back! The situation could have been prevented if Linda had asked her hostess where she might change her infant.

Admittedly, there are times when diapers must be changed in less-than-ideal places and sometimes in the presence of other people. During these awkward moments, shelter the baby as much as possible and take care of the cleanup as discreetly and efficiently as possible.

Most of us are nodding our heads, knowing that this is how we always diaper babies. We wouldn't think of being sloppy or rude or crude. But we can all think of a friend or two who could use this pep talk. Let's hope she reads this.

Daddy Does Diapers?

This is a wonderful age we're living in. As women become liberated, men are more involved in home-making. Equal respect and equal sharing of all aspects of living is becoming a yuppie concept and an acceptable lifestyle for middle-class America.

Years ago Ernie ran next door to get the neighbor to change the diaper of the child he was babysitting . . . his own child. Why do people call it "babysitting" when the father is taking care of his own children? Anyway, 20 years later we find Ernie babysitting his first grandchild and willingly handling it all. This is what we call progress!

Paul and I share all aspects of parenting. Being home all day, I obviously change the majority of diapers, but Paul is willing to learn and help out whenever he is home. Paul recognizes that both of us work very hard all day long—he at work, me at home. We are both tired at the end of a day. Once he is home, if I am cooking, Paul takes care of the baby. If the baby messes during his "on-duty" time, he draws the winning number!

"Coping" is something that both wives and husbands can learn. It's difficult for some men, and each couple must be sensitive and work out what they believe is fair in their venture together as parents. But communication on this subject might help. If you as a mother dream of having your husband involved in parenting, discuss your expectations and negotiate his level of involvement together. Each partner must be willing to sacrifice for the welfare of this baby and as a gift to the other spouse. Try to help each other through the difficult chores, then help each other enjoy the relaxing playtimes as a family. During the evening try to enjoy your husband and your baby together. You might put the child to bed together, on alternate nights. The goal is to share in your parenting.

Tedious Tasks Versus "Important Employment"

I ran down to Karen's for a cup of coffee. It's fun to

have a neighbor who will take a half-hour break with you in the middle of the morning. We share how our families are doing and what has surfaced on our "to do" list for the rest of the day. "As you can see, I'm in my *uniform*," Karen joked, referring to her jeans and a fresh blouse.

I knew what she meant. This isn't a glamorous career—and yet in many ways it is. We both enjoyed careers earlier in our lives and knew we wanted to be home full-time now. Whether we can afford the luxury of being a full-time mother, or sacrificially make full-time mothering a priority, it is imperative that we believe in what we're doing!

Priority—mothering is significant. I have *chosen* to devote myself to this task above all other careers I might pursue at this time.

Although many tasks in motherhood seem tedious and boring, we must recognize that in our former career there were also frustrating days with boring tasks to be done. The grass on the other side of the fence is not always greener. Let's see how we make the most of our tedious chores.

From My Laundry Room to Yours

Paul and I are now 17-plus years along in our marriage. Facility-wise, life is easier. We have a larger home with a large, finished laundry room. Other people brag about their cars or furs or diamonds. I brag about my laundry room. I don't think architects have any idea how much of a mother's life is lived in the laundry room.

When Paul and I were first married, we lived in apartments while he finished college. The laundry rooms were located a flight downstairs. How I remember juggling the baby on one hip and the laundry basket loaded with clothes, detergent, and fabric softener on the other hip. My hips have never been the same!

Following my days of doing laundry in coin-operated machines located an exhausting hike from our apartment, we moved to Fresno and bought our first house. This was a lovely home with beautiful landscaping and a kidney-shaped swimming pool. But the laundry area was in the garage. I spent 11 years doing laundry here, with toddlers crying in the house and me crying in the garage.

Does laundry ever affect you this way? With toddlers and babies in diapers, have you ever figured out how many hours a week you spend doing laundry? Maybe God knew He would hold my attention by keeping me doing laundry in my garage. I used to try to reason out loud with Him there: "Why, God, when young mothers have babies and toddlers, and need more bedrooms and nice laundry rooms, can they only afford small houses with depressing laundry areas? Why do You allow older couples, whose children are raised and gone, to buy huge homes with lots of bedrooms that lie vacant? Isn't life backward? Do You realize how many hours I spend out here . . . doing laundry . . . complaining to You? If You ever decide to give me a nice laundry room after the kids are all out of diapers—You can forget it."

I've since apologized to the Lord and graciously accepted my present laundry room, even though the kids are getting older and the load is half what it used to be.

I did learn some lessons doing laundry in a Laundromat and garage.

Lesson 1. When I feel defeated at a certain stage of my life—whether prompted by my physical setting or other circumstances—God gets my attention and I am teachable. I hope that I'll remain *teachable* more often so He won't have to keep getting my attention.

> "I have learned to be content in whatever circumstances I am" (Philippians 4:11).

I admit I'm a slow learner!

Lesson 2. We mothers do not see the whole picture of our lives. Our understanding is limited to the disaster of the moment.

> "Trust in the Lord with all your heart, and do not lean on your own understanding. In all your ways acknowledge Him, and He will make your paths straight" (Proverbs 3:5,6).

> "There is an appointed time for everything" (Ecclesiastes 3:1).

Lesson 3. If you *can* do something now, do it! If you have the finances for a larger home, don't wait for a rainy day. With a house full of kids, your rainy day is now!

My parents were an example to me in this area. While they were raising five children, they could afford a large home plus a summer home where we enjoyed family vacations. We also traveled extensively as a family. Now that their five daughters are married and raising families of their own, my parents have moved into a condominium. They keep the summer home for family reunions but have disposed of the extras they used to raise the five of us. Dad calls it "scaling down." He's always been so practical!

Tedious-Tasks Time

The key to living through years of "tedious tasks" is to make them as important as they need to be—but no more important. Let them take as much time as they need to take—but no more time.

Doing laundry, scrubbing toilets, and organizing closets are all important—to a point. They are important, like eating nutritiously is important. Important to your total health. Important to how you feel about yourself. Important to how good you look. Important to how well you function. But *not important enough to consume your whole day*!

Many women let tedious tasks consume their lives. They *dwell* on projects which must be done over and over again. I'm not saying that housekeeping and homemaking are not important. I *am* saying that if all your tasks are tedious you have more to offer and more creativity in you than you are using.

Many years ago I was challenged by Ann Ortlund's book *Disciplines of the Beautiful Woman*. I have applied her "elimination" and "concentration" to every area of my life. I work to *eliminate* the clutter and the unimportant and to *concentrate* on what really counts. Through much prayer and evaluation I decide where to concentrate. I don't feel guilty about not living up to another person's expectations. "Misery loves company" is not an invitation for me to lower my standards, do less thinking, and be less than God intended me to be.

Tedious tasks can be very important. I love a clean house. I love an organized home. How can we take care of these responsibilities without letting them consume us? We do it by focusing on four prerequisites:

1. A *system* for cleaning
2. A *schedule* for cleaning and laundry
3. *Security* in our priorities
4. *Flexibility* for fun!

Let's take a look at these areas one by one, so we can move on to life beyond "tedious tasks."

A System for Cleaning

Over the years I've experimented with many cleaning systems. Each woman needs to experiment until she finds what works best for her. Here are some ideas:

1. List the things that need to be done. Prioritize your list (numbering 1 to 25 or whatever), and tackle the list in order of importance. At the end of the day you've accomplished the most important tasks. This system is outlined in Marabel Morgan's book *The Total Woman*.

2. Make a 3 x 5 card file, listing each job that must be done on a file card and filing it under the appropriate day of the week. Daily *do* what the card says to do for that day!

3. Fill a "job jar" with what needs to be done and introduce the element of surprise to housecleaning responsibilities. The results are not too efficient, but you might use this system every so often and include the family in your get-caught-up campaign.

4. Hire a professional housecleaner and let her keep things spic-and-span. This works beautifully if you can afford it. But even with a professional cleaner, you need to organize and make sure your house is maintained the way you like it.

5. Set aside an allotted time each week to clean house top to bottom. I keep all of my cleaning supplies in one spot, ready for the once-a-week housecleaning. I have a "rag" box and I launder my rags each week after use, then fold them and return them to the box for the next week.

6. Begin at the front door and work your way

toward the back of the house, sorting and cleaning. If you have a lot of clutter, you could use the well-known "three-box" approach:

1. A giveaway box
2. A throwaway box
3. A storage box

The basic concept is *file, don't pile.*

A Schedule for Cleaning

If I do not set aside an allotted time to clean each week, I take much more time than is necessary. I like to decide approximately how many hours I need to clean my house (say, five hours a week) and then try to stick to that schedule. I can clean one whole day or two-half days. I do the same planning with my laundry. Then I decide what else I want to do with life (my time is my life), and I write a tentative schedule.

Your schedule will differ according to:

- when your husband leaves for work and when he comes home.
- when and if your children go to school and come home.
- if you have employment outside the home.
- whether you want to work harder in the morning or the afternoon.

A Mother's Schedule

Each year I write a reminder and a prayer at the top of my calendar: I HAVE ALL THE TIME I NEED TO DO ALL THAT GOD INTENDS ME TO DO. GOD DELIVER ME FROM THE BARRENNESS OF A BUSY LIFE.

As I evaluate my goals, I try to balance my *doing* with my *being*. It's easy to fill up 24 hours with *doing*. Too many of us mistake busyness for godliness or ful-fillment.

Bonnie Wheeler in her book *The Hurrier I Go* challenges her readers with this question: "What does God want from my time?" Time is not just for spend-ing—it's for investing. She illustrates by examining the lives of Mary and Martha. "They are two halves of the whole I want to be," she explains.

Every August (before school begins) and every January first, I find myself thinking about the new year. Before I begin creating my schedule, I list my priorities, review my long-range goals and short-term goals, and generally reevaluate what I would like to do with my life. Then I take a fresh sheet of paper and make a schedule chart with the seven days of the week across the top and the time in half-hour increments from 6 A.M. to 10 P.M. down the left side. (When I create a neat chart that I'm happy with, I make a dozen or so photocopies so I can change my schedule. I also use these blanks for my older daughters' schedules.)

First, I block in my regular weekly commitments, such as women's Bible study, employment outside the home, church activities, exercise classes, or night school courses.

Next, I fill in my children's schedules—times they need me to read to them, help them with homework or piano practice, or drive them to gymnastics classes or soccer practices.

Third, I schedule some time for my personal goals. For example, I might take the two hours during baby's naptime to work on a business that I'm running from my home.

Finally, I block in the time when I will do my house-hold chores.

When allocating time for each activity, I consider the time needed to dress or prepare and to drive to the function. If, for example, I'm planning to exercise three mornings a week, I allow time for showering and grooming after each exercise session. I try to be as realistic as possible.

If you do not work outside the home, or you are committed to full-time mothering at this stage of life, the children's naptime may hold different dreams for you. Many mothers commit this time to reading, studying, writing letters, or napping themselves. They would *never* do housework during this precious quiet time. Their sanity is important. Others feel that a clean house is top priority. They swing into action, attacking bathrooms and kitchen. Their only complaint is that when evening arrives and they want to drop from exhaustion, they still see "one more thing to do" and never find any time for themselves.

Knowing Our Priorities

Marvelous Martha worked outside the home, inside the home, on the PTA board, on the Little League committee, as wedding hostess at the church, and as room mother for her child's classroom. She even had time for women's luncheons and church women's morning coffees. One day she arrived at her Christian friend's coffee party just in time to hear her friend suggest, "Let's go around and share what the Lord has been teaching each of us in our quiet time this morning or this past week." Martha panicked. Bible study and prayer were things she always meant to do but never got around to. "These ladies would never understand," she thought. "I'm sure God would. Or would He?"

Many of us can relate to the apostle Paul's struggle in Romans 7:15. We find ourselves doing what we don't want to do, and not doing what we know would be better for us. "For the wishing is present in me, but the doing of the good is not" (Romans 7:18).

We all know that good things in life are the enemy of the best things. How do we determine what is truly best for us? We may have a few ideas, while God might be saying, "Why won't you let Me make of you what I had planned?" Let's briefly examine God's priorities and the influence they should have on our schedule.

Priority number one. "You shall have no other gods before Me" (Exodus 20:3). This is the *first* commandment, and if we're serious about obeying it, our number one priority will be to spend time reading God's Word and talking to Him each day. We need to set aside time to "be still and know that I am God" (Psalm 46:10). Jill Briscoe, in her book *Fight for the Family*, stresses that effective prayer takes time and discipline. She teases, "After we have taken time out to pray about what to pray about—we have to start to pray about it!"

In your schedule, set aside time for Bible study, prayer, and meditation. In later chapters I will share some methods I've found effective in my walk. But any method is effective only if implemented at some point in your day. If you're a morning person, a 6 A.M. study time might get your day off to its best start. If you're a groper in the morning, say a quick prayer to help you through your morning rituals and wait until the children are off to school before you sit down for your quiet time. If you will have constant interruptions until you finally get your baby or toddlers down for naps, then wait until after lunch to have that study hour. The important thing is to schedule time for it and make it your number one priority.

Priority number two. After fellowship with God, our number two reason for existence is companionship with our husband. Once we marry, we have a privilege and an obligation to share in our husband's life. Usually our husband's business or ministry takes him out of the home. We are wise to prepare a haven for him to return to. With toddlers underfoot and so much to do, we need to set aside time for quiet, relaxed dinners and romantic evenings whenever possible. Weekly dates are a treat, even if they only happen once a month! Paul and I try to keep our romantic love alive. I've decorated our bedroom as beautifully as we can afford. We try to never discuss heavy topics in the bedroom, nor do we keep any paperwork in the bedroom. Knowing that we don't agree on everything, we save this room for unity and peace. Ruth Graham was once asked whether she and her husband agreed on everything. She answered, "If Billy and I agreed on everything, one of us would be unnecessary!"

Priority number three. Motherhood ranks not first, but *third* in our lives. If we put our children above our husband, our marriage will suffer and so will our example to our children! THE GREATEST THING A MOTHER CAN DO FOR HER CHILDREN IS TO LOVE THEIR FATHER. If we put *anything* above God, everything will suffer.

Priority number four. This will vary for many people, but high on our priority list should be time for our own personal development—for reading, physical fitness, studying, and developing our minds, talents, and creativity.

I've heard it argued that *you*—your personal development, fulfillment, and fitness—should come first in life next to God and that you cannot give your best to the others unless you have taken care of your own needs first. This concept is partially true. The danger is that a woman could become too self-centered and lose perspective on servanthood (in her Christian life and as a wife and a mother). Though the women's movement has produced much good, it has also produced an equal amount of confusion. To take good care of yourself, to be a good steward of the body and mind the Lord has given you, is scriptural. To put yourself above all others is against Jesus' teaching. The Bible teaches equality. The Bible teaches that we are important to God. The Bible also teaches, and Jesus demonstrated, that we are to sacrifically care for one another and serve one another. Is this not the definition of marriage and motherhood?

Priority number five. Ministry outside the home comes only after we have ministered within the home. Our first responsibility is always to our own family's needs. Then we can reach out to the other needs around us and exercise our spiritual gifts in our church and local Christian organizations. There are many examples of Christian women who are *doers*—speaking at women's Bible studies, helping with Christian projects, baking for teas, serving at banquets—while their own families fall apart. In the list of qualifications for a Christian leader, 1 Timothy 3:4,5 says: "He must be one who manages his own household well, keeping his children under control with all dignity (but if a man does not know how to manage his own household, how will he take care of the church of God?)." Paul is speaking directly to pastors and elders, but the principle of priorities applies to all. We should take care of our own family before we minister to other people. Paul writes in the same passage, "Women must likewise be dignified, not malicious gossips, but temperate, faithful in all things" (1 Timothy 3:11).

I do believe every woman needs a ministry. The question is, How much time can you afford to serve without neglecting the needs of your family?

Jill Briscoe tells a story about growing up in England

and how her father used to take her to the wharves to see the large ships. One day Jill asked her father why a bold line was drawn around each ship's hull. Her father explained that this was the "sea level" measurement that showed how much cargo each ship could safely carry. Ships loaded so heavily that they floated below this line might sink in a storm because of too heavy a load. Ships that didn't carry any cargo were just as dangerous. A storm could toss them around because they had too little weight and stability.

We women are similar to those ships. We come in all shapes and sizes: cargo freighters, fishing boats, tiny canoes. Each size has a safety line—a "sea level" measurement—that represents a reasonable capacity for cargo (ministry workload). Some women can carry a huge load with no trouble at all. Yet all women have a sinking point. We hear the phrase "If you need something done, ask a busy woman." It's true—some women know how to work and organize, and they prove themselves reliable. But they *do* have a sinking point, and many "glub" along with heads barely above water while we expect them to do still more.

On the other hand, some women think life is a breeze. They arrive at church functions and special outings and enjoy the benefits of everyone else's hard work without contributing themselves. It seems like such a carefree life—until the storm hits. This woman can sink as quickly as the overcommitted woman because she has no stability—no roots, no solid base, no worthwhile responsibility in her life.

As women we need to share some of the cargo load. I'm a bit of a freighter myself, and I enjoy it, but I do have a limit. You have a limit too. Take on cargo or lighten your load according to what you know your capacity to be.

Priority number six. If you are employed outside the

home, you need to plan quality work and to excel in whatever God has called you to do. If you run a business from your home, you need time to run it efficiently. The Proverbs 31 woman successfully maintained her business contracts without neglecting the needs of her family. God may or may not open a door for you to become involved in some type of business venture. Whatever God does call you to do, He calls you to work within the framework of your priorities and to "let your light shine" in the workplace.

Priority number seven. You decide. Your list could go on and on. But remember that there are "seasons" of life. There may be years when all you can handle are priorities one through four, with a little of number five. Then confidently stick to your priorities and don't get bogged down with cargo ("pressure projects") that take you away from your reason for living. Later, when your children are all in school, you may be able to add to your cargo. God wants you to be fulfilled and successful. God wants you to use your talents and creativity. God wants you to trust His Word and take care of first things first, so that He can make of you what He had planned to make of you.

Flexibility for Fun

"What a gorgeous day! Let's take off for the park and lie in the sun!"

"Have you heard? Sandi Patti's coming to town for a concert. Let's get tickets and go!"

"Have you read this morning's want ads? Let's take the day off and go garage sale-ing!"

"Mommy, you promised we'd go to the zoo sometime. Why can't we go today?"

With priorities neatly listed, schedules carefully posted, and goals logged, you can become too efficient for your own good. Relax a little. Life is meant to be enjoyed. "Take time to smell the roses." Take time to laugh.

Betty was becoming known as a stick-in-the-mud. She had been invited out often but always said no because of her schedule. Her children's teachers had called, needing extra drivers for field trips, but Betty had to do her laundry. The neighbors wanted a spring "coffee get-together," but Betty was too busy with family chores. Betty was glued to her schedule to the exclusion of meeting people's needs or being sociable. There is a fine line between letting people waste your time—which they will—and being balanced and available to meet the needs of people. That's why we sometimes need *Plan B days*.

Plan A is my written schedule. Plan B is when the Lord gives me something better to do that day. In my Bible, beside Proverbs 3:27,28, I have written: "Plan B Days!" The passage says,"Do not withhold good from those to whom it is due, when it is in your power to do it. Do not say to your neighbor, 'Go, and come back, and tomorrow I will give it,' when you have it with you."

Plan B is not a cop-out to run from party to coffee klatch while you ignore your messy home and disastrous laundry room and poorly planned meals. Plan B is a way for you to be able to answer the door when opportunity knocks. Sometimes Plan B is the Lord saying, "Life is too short. You haven't been laughing as much as I'd planned. Get out and enjoy My creation today!"

Plan B activities might mean:

- An impromptu picnic
- A walk in the park
- Helping a friend with a project

- A cup of coffee on the front steps, watching your children do cartwheels on the grass
- A game of ball
- A visit to the library
- Dropping in on a friend and bringing donuts for her and her kids
- Taking a picture of your child playing "dress-up"
- Stopping for a "tickle fight"
- A luncheon out
- A game of hide-and-seek...maybe even with your husband!

Plan B activities can turn tedious days into terrific times!

4

Reasoning and Rationalizing

Tom and Tricia McFarlen are sharp, full of fun, and very popular—when they don't have their kids with them. People love to invite them to couples' parties, and people love to go out for dinner with them and other couples, but they conveniently forget to invite them over as a family—after they've done it once.

Have you ever witnessed a hurricane? When the McFarlen kids visit, there isn't a plant not overturned. Most of Junior's food never makes it to his mouth. Not all of it is ground into the carpet; some of it is used to fingerpaint down the hallway. It doesn't matter what background dinner music is played, since there isn't one moment all evening when the kids aren't screaming, wailing, or yelling "Tackle!" It's youngsters like those McFarlen rug-rats who give kids a bad name.

Must all toddlers be tagged terrors? Is "terrible two's" a mandatory stage, as advertised? Do children always ruin parties? Is it possible for children to behave in a mannerly way when they're away from home and still have a good time? Are the parents of these whirlwinds really oblivious to the chaos created by their offspring?

An even more curious question seems to arise when

the same children are observed away from their parents. Cary Incorrigible is dropped off, ready to tackle the party and the furnishings. When Mrs. Calm Authority catches his arm and explains eyeball to eyeball what the game plan is and what is totally out of bounds, Cary seems to connect. He obviously remembers his last visit and the immediate consequence that followed when he ignored Mrs. Authority's rules. He seems more at peace and secure with himself this time. Playtime goes much smoother today—almost enjoyable for Mrs. Calm Authority.

Then Cary's mother comes by to pick him up. The minute she steps into the room, Cary Incorrigible remembers his name and takes on the world—screaming, kicking, throwing toys, and causing the chaos he's used to causing. Exasperated, Mama hauls her tantrum out to the car after 11 attempts to coax him without using lasso and rope. Does she have any idea of the Jekyll and Hyde she's created? Does she even know that there's potential for peace within her child? How does Mama cope with the chaos created by her child . . . or is it created by her child? "A child who gets his own way brings shame to his mother" (Proverbs 29:15).

Every child born wants his own way. Initially he gets his way by crying, and later he learns other methods. As an infant grows and begins to walk and talk, it is our task as mothers to begin molding our child's behavior according to the principles of the Bible and the ethics of our society. First we plant seeds. Then part of our responsibility is to do some weeding!

For a baby, it's fairly obvious how to meet the physical needs: We feed him tenderly, keep him clean and dry and properly clothed, and play with him, exercising his developing muscles and reflexes.

It's obvious how to meet his spiritual needs: He's too young to be responsible for himself, so we pray for his well-being and his future.

It's fun meeting his mental needs: We talk to him eyeball to eyeball, stimulating his mind and curiosity. We play music and place bright colors around him and hang interesting mobiles to arouse his curiosity.

It's heartwarming to meet his emotional needs: pouring out love through hugs and kisses and hours of rocking and cooing this cuddly, breathing, Cabbage Patch Original.

It's when the time comes to begin meeting a child's *social* needs that we as parents often fall short. No one wants to be the bad guy—the one who has to say no. It can hurt to pull out stubborn weeds.

Social needs must be met by allowing social interaction while setting limits within each setting. *Acceptable behavior* requires evaluating a child's age and ability by the mother, then controlling what is unreasonable while enforcing what is teachable—stage by stage and age by age—until you're done! It's not an unachievable task.

Debbie Boone admitted that, as a child, she was embarrassed when her father would appear on national television and tell the world how he spanked his daughters, and later wouldn't let them date until they were 16. Debbie in a conversation with our mutual friend Stan said, "Today I treasure the restrictions my parents put on me. I'm so grateful that they were strict with me." Debbie is now the mother of a son, Jordan, and twin daughters, Gabrielle and Dustin. She knows the value of a disciplined upbringing. The Boones planted disciplined seeds and saw that they reaped later than they sowed and more than they had sowed. Debbie's parents have reached the goal of having their children "rise up and call them blessed."

In reasoning the how's and why's of proper discipline, my mind goes back to the four years when

I taught elementary school before becoming a mother. I taught fifth grade and was Music Specialist at Bannatyne Elementary School in St. James (Winnipeg), Canada. Each year when our choir of nearly 200 voices competed in the Manitoba Music Festival, I could count on even my rebel terrorists to behave well in public and perform beautifully on stage for the judges and audience. Even Reggie, a "problem child" whom other teachers warned I should not put in my choir, arrived on competition day with clean face, slicked-down hair, and a desire to please. Was this the same kid who repeated grades, kicked down doors, punched out peers on the playground, and vocalized every swear word I'd ever heard before he began vocalizing with my choir? What made the difference? The principles that worked then work today in my job of mothering. All children need to know who is in charge and to experience consistency.

Children Need to Know Who Is the Authority

In any organization there needs to be *order*. Whether we're organizing a classroom, a choir, a youth group, or a family, there needs to be a leader—an authority—a commander-in-chief. In this day and age of free expression, we still cannot function and progress without order and leadership.

A choir is a good example: Each singer has a favorite song, a best key, a most enjoyable rhythm, a unique harmony. Creativity is wonderful. But to function as a choir, a leader (director) needs to dictate what will be sung, in what key, at what tempo, with a predetermined harmony. He needs to lead the group, following the choices (rules) that he has determined are best for the group as a whole. Individuals must conform.

So it is with whatever group we are asked to lead—

including our family. There must be a set of rules predetermined by you, pertaining to what you will do and when you will do it. Then you need to go ahead and lead! Don't wait for someone else to do it. *You're* the leader.

When I taught public school, I could easily tell which students came from homes where Mom and Dad were the leaders. They knew how to listen and obey. They did not know what the word "submission" meant, but they got an "A" in it.

For many years my husband was a youth pastor, and I assisted him with many youth activities, Bible studies, and youth choirs. Here again, I could easily tell which young people came from homes where Dad and Mom were the authorities. These teens were alive and fun-loving, but they submitted to leadership at the appropriate times and were a joy to direct and discipline. The opposite was also true: The rude and disrespectful teens reflected badly on their parents.

The seeds of authority and discipline have long-term effects. They can determine how well a person functions in his or her job. For three years Paul and I owned a clothing store in California. We hired many teenage girls to work for us. Some of them knew how to work and submit to leadership, and some of them did not. Inevitably, those who had bad attitudes, who showed up late, and who had poor work habits came from homes where they did not learn to submit to authority.

The young child who never learns to obey his parent often becomes the student who will not obey his teacher and later will not follow his youth director's leadership. As a teen he disobeys his employer. Eventually he may go against the authority of the law, and throughout his entire life he never learns to submit to God. An entire life can be wasted because a child did not learn to submit. God has a lot to say about authority:

At home: "Honor your father and your mother" (Exodus 20:12). "Children, obey your parents in the Lord, for this is right" (Ephesians 6:1).

At school: "A pupil is not above his teacher" (Matthew 10:24).

At church: "Remember those who led you, who spoke the word of God to you; and considering the result of their conduct, imitate their faith" (Hebrews 13:7).

At work: "Servants (employees), be submissive to your masters (employers) with all respect, not only to those who are good and gentle, but also to those who are unreasonable" (1 Peter 2:18).

To police and government: "Let every person be in subjection to the governing authorities.... Therefore he who resists authority has opposed the ordinance of God" (Romans 13:1,2).

To God: "Submit therefore to God" (James 4:7).

Children Need Consistency

"Who's the boss of this family?" may not be what your toddler verbalizes, but that's what he's evaluating. When you yell "Don't touch!" your diapered darling wants to know, "Do you mean now or do I get four more times before I have to quit?"

If you answer "That depends," you as a parent haven't decided the rules to the game you're teaching your youngster. So how do you expect him to play without cheating? With a creative mind and a will to challenge any obstacle in his path, the child can innocently take you on and you'll both end up losers. The game of life does have some absolute rules. In teaching your child the rules, be consistent in your reinforcement.

Consistent Verbal Reinforcement

From an early age a child needs to be told that Daddy is the head of the home and that next to Daddy, Mommy is the head of the home. Among the first verses I had my children memorize were Ephesians 6:1, "Children, obey your parents in the Lord, for this is right," and Ephesians 6:2, "Honor your father and mother."

Verbally stating the chain of command is the start of good communication and teaching obedience. Be very open about the fact that you and your husband must both submit to God, and that your children must submit to you because God commands it in the Bible.

Consistent Modeling

As your children grow older they will see this mutual love and submission and will learn more from your modeling than they will from your verbalizing. True modeling of love and submission has become nearly obsolete in America. Through years of seeking liberation many women have thrown out the baby with the bathwater. And they've literally lost their families as a result. Lately we find a number of progressive mothers realizing that God's absolutes are liberating and that the only way back to true success as a mother is to follow God's rules. I encourage you not to groan over the Victorian misunderstandings that might have been forced on you, but to study God's Word for yourself. Let Him give you a fresh picture of His plan for you and your child. *Know* what you believe. Day by day stick to these principles as you teach them to your child, and more importantly as you model them for your child.

Consistent Physical Reinforcement

In rearing young children this is probably the most controversial issue: TO SPANK OR NOT TO SPANK? Having researched authors in both camps and interviewed families on opposing sides, I still firmly believe that there is a time and a place where physical discipline is the most effective and the quickest means of changing an undesirable action.

> "He who spares his rod hates his son, but he who loves him disciplines him diligently" (Proverbs 13:24).

> "Foolishness is bound up in the heart of a child; the rod of discipline will remove it far from him" (Proverbs 22:15).
> "Do not hold back discipline from the child; although you beat him with the rod, he will not die" (Proverbs 23:13).

Before I encourage you to use physical discipline in training your young child, I must first cry out against our nation's terrible problem of child abuse. This abuse is committed by parents in all races and socioeconomic levels, and even in some Christian homes. Children are hit rather than spanked and beaten rather than trained. As a result they are broken both physically and emotionally. Some children physically die when their emotionally disturbed parents lose control. Others die emotionally as their parents shout and hurl verbal abuse at them.

The key to discipline is *control*. Control should be the core of physical discipline. A parent should always model self-control and should never discipline in anger.

Physical discipline and child abuse have nothing in common. The first is of God and the other is of Satan. One is because of love and the other is because of hate. The most important aspect of physical discipline is our attitude:

> "Fathers (mothers), do not provoke your children to anger; but bring them up in the discipline and instruction of the Lord" (Ephesians 6:4).

Authority needs to be filled with *affection* to obtain the results that God purposed for discipline. If you are not *motivated by love*, you should not be disciplining.

When to Use Corporal Punishment

Karin was helping her mom do the dishes. Bryan and Jeffrey were out playing hockey while little Erik toddled through the kitchen. In big-sister fashion, Karin tossed a ball to Erik, who tossed it back. Karin, leaping to catch it, knocked over her mom's expensive crystal pitcher, which shattered into a hundred pieces. What should Mom do? Is a spanking in order?

No. Even though Karin acted irresponsibly, this was an accident. She did not willfully break the pitcher. She wasn't trying to disobey.

She might have to help clean up, or babysit Erik while Mom cleans up, and then she might have to decide how she will help pay for the loss.

"You play, you pay" can be taught from a very young age. Working to repair or replace or make up for an error is known as *restitution*. Many examples of this can be cited from Scripture. Here is one of them:

> "Then it shall be, when he sins and becomes guilty, that he shall restore what he took by robbery, or what he got by extortion, or the deposit which was entrusted to him, or the lost thing which he found" (Leviticus 6:4).

Exodus 22 also defines the law of restitution.

Let's contrast this with another situation. Michael picked up his dad's empty coffee mug and lifted his arm to hurl it like a football across the living room. Dad ran and grabbed it out of his hand. "No, no Michael! DO NOT TOUCH MY COFFEE CUP! We never play with coffee mugs or any dishes, and we never throw anything in the living room. Do you understand me?" Michael nodded, waited a few minutes until his dad's back was turned, then hurled the mug across the living room. Luckily, it landed up on the couch and didn't break. Should Michael be spanked?

Absolutely! He *willfully disobeyed* Dad. He purposefully *challenged authority.*

In *Dare to Discipline*, James Dobson suggests that when a child expresses a defiant "I will not" or "You shut up," this is not the time to have a discussion about the virtues of obedience, nor should you send him to his room to pout. You have drawn a line in the dirt, and your child has deliberately placed his foot across it. The question is, "Who's in charge here?" The only other time I feel that spanking is absolutely necessary is in regard to *safety.* If your child steps off the curb onto the street, he gets spanked. Teach it once and then consistently reinforce it.

How to Use Corporal Punishment

1. As soon as possible after the willful defiance, the child should be punished. The whole point of the spanking is to impress upon the child's mind that the

deed is wrong and must not occur again. Keeping the punishment close in time to the wrongful act reinforces the *cause and effect* that we're teaching. A word of caution: If you need time to cool down so as not to spank in anger, send your child to his room while you sit quietly for a minute and pray for composure.

2. Discipline in a private place. Never allow siblings or friends to watch or hear. If you are away from home, go to a restroom or out to your car or to some other private place. Embarrassment is not part of the punishment; that will damage the spirit. The conflict is between *your authority* and *your child's obedience.* Preserving your child's dignity and good self-esteem is as important as the disciplining process. So mold the will but never break the spirit.

3. Enter the room *calmly,* and then *briefly* review what the child did wrong so he knows why you're punishing him. This is not a plea-bargaining time. Your client is already sentenced.

4. Use a neutral object if possible. The Bible speaks of the "rod." Whether we apply a wooden spoon, spanking stick, ruler, paddle, or leather belt, it is the object causing the child pain by direct contact. Some scholars claim that the human hand should be reserved for loving, and that if a child is disciplined properly with a spanking object, he will not pull back when his mother's arm is raised at other times.

5. Have the child lie over your knee or flat on his bed—hands above his head—or stand bending over and grasping his knees. Then firmly spank the child on the buttocks. The spanking must cause immediate sharp pain, yet not bruise or damage the child in any way. You must use good judgment in determining how hard to swing. Diaper-padded toddlers need to feel some kind of a jolt through all their layers or else it is not worth the effort. Older children can try to

outsmart their parents. Once Jan didn't seem to be in much pain following her swat. Seconds later it was discovered that she had reinforced her pants with soft-covered books. It's difficult to discipline a genius! Cheryl used to giggle from nervousness. The more Paul spanked Cheryl, the more she laughed, even though she was hurting. In that kind of situation, only you can determine when you've done all that you can or should.

6. When the spanking is over, allow some time for crying (maybe for both of you) and then spend some time loving. Tell your child how much you love him and that because of this you need to teach him to obey authority and behave correctly. You can reinforce what the proper behavior is, but always end on the note of how much you love him. If the child is a toddler, hold him in your arms so he can feel your affection and won't be afraid of you. If the child is older, this might be a good time for a discussion of why kids get in trouble and how important values are. If there needs to be forgiveness—on your part or the child's—take care of this immediately. Always end the session by showing love to your child.

The advantage of using corporal discipline during the first three years is that you get a lot of training completed before the child can consciously remember it!

Results of Consistent Discipline

Our children can sit quietly for hours at a fine restaurant and enjoy listening to adult conversation while they draw and quietly chatter between themselves. People sometimes stop by our table and ask us how we do it. It's very simple. We clearly explain to the children what type of behavior we expect. If and when the child disobeys (they all try it once or twice), he is quietly removed, taken outside the restaurant for a firm spanking (no feeble swats), and brought back in. They know we mean business. They know we will enforce what we say. Therefore, they obey. The results are that they feel secure in our parenting and they actually feel pride in their good behavior, especially when observers compliment them!

I need to mention here that children can't *always* be quiet. These times of strict behavior are saved for special occasions. They are balanced with daily play and fun and physical sports where "noise" is allowed and even enjoyed. Balance is the key to all of living and a key to teaching children to behave.

Consistent Consistency!

This is the most difficult thing for me—being consistently consistent. I know what I want my children to know and I know how I want them to obey, but there are days when I want to say, "Do what you like. I'm too pooped to pull myself out of this chair to give you the punishment you deserve. Forget the rules for now. I'll pretend I don't see or hear until I'm rested and feeling better." The result of such negligence is that children's sins expand like leavened bread dough. By the time I get around to handling the sin, it has doubled or quadrupled. Then I really need a double or quadruple burst of energy to knead the dough.

My goal is to keep up-to-date with my children day by day. I pray for consistency, I pray for wisdom, and I pray for love.

Possible Parenting Patterns

Whether we are contrasting the liberal versus the restrictive, the authoritarian versus the permissive, or the authoritative versus the responsible parent, we all want to find the happy medium. We want to be parents who teach each child, discipline each child, disciple each child to accept responsibility, and love each child unconditionally, thereby assuring the child that he is capable and loved. Dr. Kevin Leman in his book *Making Children Mind Without Losing Yours* contrasts the different styles of parenting. The authoritarian mother is extremely strict, controlling the child's life as much as possible. This parent thinks she is taking such good care of the child, but the child feels he is in jail and may never be allowed to grow up and make his own decisions. This child often resorts to outrageous rebellion or a sneaky double life in order to gain his own identity.

The permissive mother wants to be the child's pal. She lets the child do whatever he wants and always helps when the child has any problem. This "nice" mother actually teaches her child to make immature decisions and soon discovers that there is no respect between the child and herself. Instead of being liked, Mom becomes a pitiful pushover.

Whether we call the overbearing mother authoritarian or aggressive, she oversteps the bounds of respect and dignity due every human being.

Whether we call the insecure mother permissive or passive, she fears using the authority invested in her by God to be a parent.

Once we understand our position as parents, we begin to reason and rationalize.

Let's examine what's reasonable and unreasonable. Some reasoning and rationalizing is good, while some is detrimental.

Reasonable Reasoning

1. To understand a mother is to be a mother. Mothering is a tough job. I am not perfect and will never be

a perfect mother. But I will do the best job I can do with the knowledge available to me and in the society in which I live.

2. I could not choose my own physical characteristics or abilities. Neither can I choose my child's physical characteristics or abilities. I acknowledge that God created us according to His will with His own expectations for me and my child. He alone understands me fully. He knows where I excel. He knows my child's limitations. I do not have to be "Super Mom" in other people's eyes. God is my maker and my judge. He does not expect more of me or my child than what He planned. He also does not expect less of me or my child!

> "Through the grace given to me I say to every man among you not to think more highly of himself than he ought to think, but to think so as to have sound judgment, as God has allotted to each a measure of faith" (Romans 12:3).

God wants us to have healthy self-images because God has allotted faith and abilities to each one of us. God also wants us to have healthy and reasonable images (thoughts) when it comes to motherhood.

Unreasonable Reasoning

1. To compare one child with another child is unreasonable and unscriptural. Each child is a unique creation.

> "Thou didst form my inward parts; Thou didst weave me in my mother's womb. I will give thanks to Thee, for I am fearfully and wonderfully made; wonderful are Thy works, and my soul knows it very well. My frame

was not hidden from Thee, when I was made
in secret, and skillfully wrought in the depths
of the earth. Thine eyes have seen my
unformed substance; and in Thy book they
were all written, the days that were ordained
for me, when as yet there was not one of
them" (Psalm 139:13-16).

Each child is uniquely gifted.

"He has filled them with skill" (Exodus 35:35).

". . . every skillful person in whom the Lord
had put skill" (Exodus 36:2).

When we compare our children to other people's
children, or compare one child with another child
within our own family, this is unreasonable reasoning. Each child is different.

If a child with average mental ability is receiving B's
and C's, praise him with words of encouragement. We
should understand our children well enough to know
whether they are capable of straight A's or whether
they need a remedial learning program. Let's be realistic about our children's abilities, using the slogan "Be
the best that *you* can be!"

2. To evaluate a child by outward physical appearance is unreasonable reasoning. Mothers who have
absolutely beautiful children can put far too much
value on the outward appearance and sometimes ruin
an otherwise likable child.

"Man looks at the outward appearance, but
the Lord looks at the heart" (1 Samuel 16:7).

I believe that everyone should look the very best he
can without misusing his time or money. However,

it's easy to place *overemphasis* on the outward appearance.

When we had our first two daughters, we absolutely loved dressing them in ribbons and lace and ruffly dresses with patent leather shoes. Fussing in front of a mirror is part of growing up for a little girl.

Our third daughter was born just as beautiful and lovable, but with a large, swollen birthmark on the bridge of her nose. It was the result of a hemangioma, a type of blood tumor. Hemangiomas are not uncommon, but they usually appear on less seen parts of the body! I used to ask the Lord, "Why couldn't this be on her bottom?"

Of course we took Deanna to pediatricians, dermatologists, and plastic surgeons. They all agreed that surgery could eventually correct it, but that we should wait five years until the blood could be absorbed.

With our first two daughters, we got used to frequent comments about their beautiful appearance. With Deanna, people would gasp or stare. They would point to the birthmark and ask, "What happened to her? Was she in an accident? Did something fall on her face?"

Realizing that she would have to live with this for several years, we began focusing on her mental and emotional well-being. As with Melanie and Cheryl, we dressed her in ribbons and lace and ruffly dresses with patent leather shoes. As we fussed with her curls, we told her, "God made you so special. We love you so much. You look so beautiful."

Because of our positive reinforcement, Deanna felt secure in who she was and secure in her Creator, knowing that He had created her special for a purpose. She would sing with our family when we did family concerts at churches in California. We would explain a little about Deanna's birthmark (to avoid a thousand questions after the concert) and then Deanna would sing a solo:

> I'm something special—
> I'm the only one of my kind.
> God gave me a body
> and a bright, healthy mind.
> He has a special purpose
> that He wanted me to find,
> So He made me something special—
> I'm the only one of my kind.*

There wouldn't be a dry eye in the sanctuary. We would let her quote John 3:16 and sing "The Books of the Bible" clearly and distinctly (which awed audiences when she was only 3½ years old). Then she sang:

> In His time, in His time,
> He makes all things beautiful in His time.
> Lord, please show me every day
> That You're teaching me Your way
> and You'll do just what You say
> in Your time.†

During those five years our whole family learned that beauty is more than what is seen at first glance. The quality of a person can be overlooked because of a handicap. We took a fresh look at how we respond to other people—whether they are in a wheelchair or deformed or blessed with beauty. We learned a lot

---

* "You're Something Special," by William J. and Gloria Gaither, © Copyright 1974 by William J. Gaither. *All rights reserved. Used by permission of Gaither Music Company.*
† "In His Time," by Diane Ball, © 1978 by Maranatha! Music. *All rights reserved. International copyright secured. Used by permission only.*

from how people responded to Deanna and how she replied. When someone would ask her, "Did you have an accident?" she would smile and say, "No. God made me special."

Sometimes people's insensitivity hurt deeply. From a distance, people would call to me and say, "Your little girl stuck a wad of gum on her nose" or "Your little girl put a grape on her nose." Others would stare angrily at me, thinking that I was an abusive parent or that I did not take care of my child. One woman called me and told me that Deanna was suffering because of sin in my life, and that if I would confess it, Deanna would be healed. That really hurt! Still, I refused to dwell on these negatives lest they hurt Deanna more.

I have no idea how many lives Deanna touched. The lesson many people learned is not to judge a book by its cover. Don't judge a human being by looking on the outward appearance. Every child is beautiful and capable and worthwhile.

Reasonable Rationalizing

1. My child is not perfect and will not behave perfectly all the time. A child is a child, he cannot behave as an adult. A child is a person; he cannot behave as an angel. Though I am a strict parent, with enforced rules and guidelines, I must realize a child's limitations. As mothers we often exclaim, "Act your age!" They usually do!

> "When I was a child, I used to speak as a
> child, think as a child, reason as a child"
> (1 Corinthians 13:11).

Children can be taught to be polite and obedient, but

they must still be allowed to be children. This is the only childhood they get! There should be time for fun and games and hours of play. Time for dreaming and using their imaginations. Time for laughing and giggling. Time for whatever appeals to them, within the guidelines of safety and your rules for politeness and obedience.

2. My child has a unique temperament and personality, and therefore may have difficulty conforming to certain requirements. Whether you're hooked on Tim and Beverly La Haye's Four Temperaments, or Type A and Type B personality traits, or Linda Yohn's Left Brain/Right Brain tendencies, you will acknowledge that each child is unique. We should observe, study, and try to understand our child's strengths and weaknesses. This helps us to encourage and mold them. This is not a cop-out for unacceptable behavior. Understanding, yes; excuse, no. As mothers we are responsible to continually train our children to obey and mature, accepting responsibility within their capabilities. All temperaments, all personalities, all "brains" are to strive to be more Christlike in character, action, and attitude.

Unreasonable Rationalizing

1. Other mothers are doing a worse job than I am. Kids today are disobedient and rebellious. It's a hopeless cause. Why should I waste my effort and energy?

> "Train up a child in the way he should go, and even when he is old he will not depart from it" (Proverbs 22:6).

We are commanded by God to train our child! "In the way he should go" might refer to his abilities, talents, and gifts, and it might also refer to his temperament, personality, and mental ability. We'll tackle more specifics of this training in Chapters 5 through 8.

2. It is inappropriate to spank or discipline my child in public or when company is over. The key to well-behaved children is *consistent consistency*. When company is over or you are in public is usually the time when a child decides to test you. He wants to know how serious you are about your rules. One or two *consistent consistencies* usually cures the problem.

Melanie was told to straighten up and talk quietly but continued to put on a show for the rest of the restaurant patrons that day. Paul warned her as to the behavior we expected and the discipline if she did not obey. She did not respond, so Paul quietly picked her up and took her out to the car for more than a talk. Paul gave her a hearty spanking. There were tears, then loving and a restating of the correct behavior that was being taught. It worked like magic. Paul and I always feel bad when we have to do this, but the principles work and Melanie did learn how to behave when taken to a restaurant.

As Melanie and Cheryl grew older, they became pros at restaurant life. Little Deanna had not yet completed the course. She began to fuss and misbehave in a favorite restaurant of ours. Paul stood up to take her out when Melanie and Cheryl chimed in, "No, please don't spank her. She didn't mean it. She didn't know what she was doing. She's sorry." We laughed. We were pleased that they wanted to defend their baby, but each child must learn for herself.

Consistency takes effort. Paul and I sometimes catch ourselves defending the child ourselves. When we sit down in a restaurant we don't feel like getting up and disciplining a child. But the rewards are worth it.

"A stitch in time saves nine"
inspires me to

"Spank when they're young and then we'll be done."

As in gardening, when we keep up with weeding day by day, it's possible to maintain an orderly garden with minimal effort as our seed grows. If we neglect the seed, and the weeds begin to overtake the garden, the task to restore order becomes an overwhelming burden.

"Weed a little each day is what I really want to say."

Enough of the negatives. Now let's move on to the good stuff.

5

Prayer, Praise, and Productivity

Why pray when you can worry? Every mother shoots up 30-second prayers to get her through the tension of the moment. It relieves some of the stress and helps her cope. But doesn't every mother know that *worry* is part of her job description? These are some of my "prayers." See how many you can relate to:

> "Please don't let my child..." "You wouldn't let that happen to me, would You? My life would be over. It wouldn't be fair to the child." "If there really is a God these things wouldn't happen. How can He allow tragedies? Doesn't He care?"

And then, as my stomach is in a knot, I think, "I wonder if other mothers worry as much as I do." For many women this hodgepodge of worry and calling out to God followed by more worry constitutes their prayer life. Talk about stress! What's the solution?

> "Be anxious for nothing, but in everything by prayer and supplication with thanksgiving let your requests be made known to God" (Philippians 4:6).

We women are never at a loss for words when it comes to making our requests known. We've got "wish lists" and "things we need" lists and mental lists of changes we'd like to see. But somehow we fail to grasp the first part of the verse. The "Be anxious for nothing—don't worry" part doesn't seem to work. Is the problem with God or is the problem within us? I'd prefer not to answer this on the grounds that it might incriminate me.

Sure I pray, but I worry that God might not do it my way. "If I totally gave the problem over to God, what would happen?" I think. "I mean, if I really prayed believing, and mentally and emotionally handed God the whole mess, what would happen?"

> "The peace of God, which surpasses all comprehension, shall guard your hearts and your minds in Christ Jesus" (Philippians 4:7).

What mother wouldn't like to live in peace? So praying with my fist open, my heart (emotionally) open, and my mind (mentally) open is the answer? That's right! It's prayer with no strings attached. It's waiting to see what God wants me to do. It's waiting for His timing, or doing what He has told me to do. The following saying helps me with raising my children: PRAY AS IF EVERYTHING DEPENDED ON GOD. OBEY AS IF EVERYTHING DEPENDED ON YOU.

If God does tell me to do something by putting an idea in my mind and tugging at my heart to follow through—this is the Holy Spirit working to direct my life—then I must do it!

Prayer can be an excuse for no action.

Sometimes the greatest prayer is, "What would You have me do, Lord?" In praying and waiting, or praying and obeying, we are to totally trust God for the results. That prevents worry—or stress—from hindering our lives.

Praying is a mother's greatest possibility. Let's examine how we can pray for our children. Once again, let's start at the beginning.

Pray for Your Child

1. *Pray for your child before he or she is born.* Most women, when they first discover they are pregnant, have a fresh awareness of God. They sense the miracle of the life within them. They sense the responsibility. They sense the lack of control in creating this new human being, and therefore turn to God, who alone decides and controls creation. They pray for a healthy, normal baby. God understands a mother's heart.

"Delight yourself in the Lord, and He will give you the desires of your heart" (Psalm 37:4). Some Christians think this is a "trick" verse: If they delight in the Lord, He will change the desires of their hearts so they'll accept what He was going to give them in the first place. I don't believe God is out to manipulate us. He gave us freedom of choice in the first place. IIe also created us to have fellowship with Him. If we *do* seek God in our lives, and truly delight ourselves in the Lord, we will follow God's perfect will for our lives and will acknowledge His perfect choices for us. Trust, faith, and understanding are all involved in the prayer of a godly woman. God does touch our hearts and change our desires as we mature in Him. God is also the final authority in what is best for us. We have to trust Him with that. But He does hear our prayers and care about our dreams.

Before our baby is born, we might pray for a boy or a girl. Our preference might be the desire of our heart (or our husband's heart), but not God's perfect choice for us. Let's not fight God (a waste of emotional effort). Let God be God. Let's delight in what He has given us. I fear that husbands need this exhortation more often than wives.

The day I delivered Cheryl, our second-born, my roommate in the hospital was a gal who had also just delivered her second daughter. She had stayed in the recovery room sleeping because she had a C-section. When she was wheeled back to our room, she found a note from her husband saying he had to go on a pressing business trip and would be back in a few days. She cried as she read the note, saying, "He really wanted a boy." I was furious. It wasn't her fault that she didn't deliver a boy. Didn't her husband know that biologically the male-determining chromosome came from his sperm? Didn't he realize that God alone controls creation? "He couldn't be a Christian," I concluded. "Not this selfish creep."

Later, as the woman and I talked, I learned that they were both born-again Christians and members of a wonderful church in town. I felt sorrow with this dear mother who should have been rejoicing on this wonderful day.

Many times over the years I've observed more celebrating over the birth of a boy than over the birth of a girl. I've seen this prejudice carry to the second generation, where grandson's births were more celebrated than granddaughter's births. To me this is primitive thinking and spiritual immaturity.

It's all right as humans to feel disappointment. But we can get over it quickly as we turn to Scripture for our standards and acknowledge God's will in our lives. Before our third daughter was born, I had prayed for a son for Paul—it seemed the right thing to do—if it was God's will. It obviously was not. And Paul, a mature Christian father, has shown how geniunely thrilled he is with each of his daughters. They feel secure in his acceptance.

My father was a wonderful example to Paul and me. He had *five* daughters and he was enthusiastic about us. Not once did he make us feel unaccepted or unappreciated. He understood "feminine equality" long before it was popular. He taught us to become all that we could become. He taught us to be confident and successful women at home, at school, at church, and in our careers.

As girls we learned to drive a tractor, participate in a debate, maneuver a speedboat, help with the hammering in constructing our summer home, participate in a prayer meeting, compete in sports, and still enjoy our femininity. Dad wanted his girls to look pretty and show that they were happy with who God created them to be. Our confidence and positive self-image are largely due to our dad's encouragement.

When praying for your child before he or she is born, pray for his future life, his future mate, his career, and his ministry. Most of all pray that he or she will accept Jesus Christ at an early age.

> "He hears the prayer of the righteous"
> (Proverbs 15:29).

2. *Pray for your child as you train him.* Praying for your child is a form of private dedication. Samuel is a miraculous story of God hearing the prayer of a mother.

> "It came about in due time, after Hannah had conceived, that she gave birth to a son; and she named him Samuel, saying, 'Because I have asked him of the Lord' " (1 Samuel 1:20).

> "For this boy I prayed, and the Lord has

given me my petition which I asked of Him.
So I have also dedicated him to the Lord; as
long as he lives he is dedicated to the Lord"
(1 Samuel 1:27,28).

"The boy Samuel was growing in stature and
in favor both with the Lord and with men"
(1 Samuel 2:26).

Dedicating your child to the Lord is an important
expression of your priorities and goals. Private dedication is significant, but public dedication in a church
service can crystallize your desires and help you visualize, acknowledge, and remember your commitment
to God.

Infant dedication is really *parent dedication*:

- The parents acknowledge the child as a gift
  from God, created by God and given to
  them to raise.
- The parents acknowledge their desire to
  dedicate this child to the Lord, praying that
  the child will accept Jesus as his personal
  Savior and will live his life for God.
- The parents acknowledge that they will
  work to raise the child by the principles in
  God's Word.
- The parents acknowledge that they will
  seek to model a godly life.
- The parents publicly declare by this baby
  dedication that they have made these
  decisions and desire the prayer and support
  of the church in raising this child for the
  Lord.

As you raise your child, you need to continue to pray
for him each day, so that as he grows in stature he

will also grow "in favor both with the Lord and with men" (1 Samuel 2:26). Also pray for yourself daily as a parent. You need strength, wisdom, discernment, love, and patience!

3. *Pray for your child during his student years.* Once your child is off to school you are not off the hook. You are still the mother. You are still responsible. You have decided *where* your child will receive his education and who will educate him. Pray for him, for his teachers, for his classmates and friends. (Peers teach more than we want them to.) Pray for all the influences in your child's life.

4. *Pray for your child for the rest of his life!* Once a mother, always a mother. When you have poured your life into another human being, you care about that life. Even after you have done all that you can, and the child has left home, you still care. So still pray, no matter what his age or circumstance in life.

Pray With Your Child

1. *Pray with your child before meals.* This is the easiest time to pray together. Jesus is our example in praying to God to say "thank You" before we eat. Matthew 15:36 talks of His feeding the four thousand: "He took the seven loaves and the fish; and *giving thanks,* He broke them and started giving them." Similar instances can be found in Mark 6:41; 8:7; 14:22; and Luke 24:30.

Romans 14:6 says, "He who eats, does so for the Lord, for he gives thanks to God."

Our family prays before every meal, even in restaurants. One reason is that we want our children to be consistent and open about their relationship with the Lord. In Acts 27:35 Paul "took bread and gave thanks to God *in the presence of all*; and he broke it and began to eat." I do believe manners are important, so I do not like a big "to-do" about it. A quiet bowing of the head and prayer of thanks is sufficient, and is a wonderful testimony to those around us.

2. *Pray with your child before school.* As my kids leave each morning they give me a quick hug and kiss and I give them a quick prayer. "Lord, help Cheryl to do well in her math test today and to have a good day with her friends. Amen." "Have a great day!" SLAM!

"Lord, help Deanna not to talk so much in school today and bless Miss Shima as she teaches these first-graders. Help Deanna to have fun in physical education. Amen." "Have a wonderful day." SLAM!

"Father, junior high years are tough. Help Melanie to rely on You for direction and not be pulled down by some of her peers. May she lift them up so they'll see You. Amen." "Love you, Melanie. Have a fun day." SLAM!

3. *Pray with your child during family devotions.* This is the time to let *them* pray, even it it's only a sentence prayer. Let them share prayer requests. Chapter 9 will provide some specific ideas for these family adventures.

4. *Pray with your child spontaneously—as problems arise.* My children are always open to praying as we drive to the dentist's office. In fact, you've never seen such enthusiasm for prayer!

5. *Pray with your child before bedtime.* I wish I could say that every night of my child's life I have knelt with them by their bed and prayed with them before I tucked them in and gave them a good-night kiss.

I started out right. Most nights I knelt and prayed by each child's crib when they were tiny. As the kids grew, I prayed many evenings for *me*. "Lord, help me to get them all to sleep. Please!"

Because my norm is not my ideal, I still strive for my ideal. Evenings when I am home and the homework is done on time and I can get each girl to bed on time, I pray with each child as I tuck her in. I wish that happened every night.

Pray Using a Notebook

Whether we use a separate prayer notebook or a section in our "life" journal, I believe we need to get something down in black-and-white to enhance our prayer life.

1. *Pray using a notebook for organization.* In my notebook I have a "Prayer" chapter that contains special people and ministries I pray for Monday through Friday. I also have a chapter in my notebook for each child. I list my goals for the child and areas we are working on. I use these pages as prayer sheets also. Then I have pages for specific prayer requests with these column headings:

> Date
> Prayer Request
> Date Answered & Comments

I believe in spontaneous prayer and that the Holy Spirit will bring to mind whom I should pray for. I also believe in organized prayer to motivate me and to expand my prayer life.

2. *Pray using a notebook for encouragement.* When I record my prayers, dated and later answered, I am encouraged that God does answer prayer! As a result, my faith is strengthened. I grow spiritually. And I encourage other people to pray too.

3. *Pray using a notebook for verification.* How soon we forget! Did I really have a terrible problem disciplining my child last year? Did God answer my prayer for wisdom and consistency? How about that financial crisis we faced? Did God really meet our needs? My notebook helps me remember.

Besides listing and dating my prayers, I often write out prayers to the Lord. I have kept these prayers for years, hidden away because they are so personal. When I get them out and reread what I prayed, I am astounded at how God answered. I forget how awful I felt and how desperate I was. But there it is in black-and-white: verification—proof that I poured out my heart to God and He provided for my need and led me through the situation.

Recently I reread the prayers I wrote when Deanna was facing surgery on her nose. We had waited nearly five years. We had prayed for God's timing. But when Dr. Jacobs of Stanford Hospital told us it was time, and we should schedule Deanna's surgery in Fresno, we had *no* medical insurance, for Paul was between jobs. The doctor's "prepayment" percentage emptied our savings account. If this operation had been for me I would have postponed it. But this was for our child, and every mother wants the best for her child.

"His time" was also an answer to prayer because we had prayed that the doctors would do the surgery before Deanna began school. Peer ridicule can be so cruel. The surgery was scheduled for March and Deanna wouldn't start school until September. Her scar would be healed. "His perfect timing" was so evident—except for our lack of medical insurance. What was God trying to teach us now?

In Paul's ministry we have sat with many families at hospitals during their children's surgeries. We thought we knew how they felt—but we really didn't.

It hurts so much. We stayed with Deanna as she was prepped for the surgery. Then we waited. The hour she was in surgery was an hour of pain and an hour of miracles—physically and financially!

This chapter is about prayer, but to be honest Paul and I did not pray out loud that hour. We hurt too much. We had prayed plenty before—when we could. We sat together in silence trying to sip a cup of coffee.

After about 15 minutes Paul decided to call Melanie and Cheryl, who were at home getting ready for school. When he came back he reported, "I just sold our old grand piano. We have cash to completely pay for Deanna's surgery, including the hospital bill!"

A few months before, we had put our old piano up for sale after buying a new one. However, it had not sold. That morning a couple who had seen it called the house at seven to make an offer. The girls took the message. Paul returned their call and settled on a price that pleased them—and it totally covered Deanna's medical expenses. What couple would call at seven A.M. to buy a piano? The exact hour Deanna was in the operating room! The exact day we needed the money! These people knew nothing of Deanna's surgery or our financial need. But God knew and He provided. God kept this "savings account" for us without our realizing it. I recorded all of this in my prayer journal, and years later it will still be there, when I'm starting to worry and need a reminder that *God answers prayer*!

Praise and Productivity

My parents have always told me "You can do it, Carol" and I've always believed them!

Many parents say things like "You're not smart enough for that," "How do you think you can pull that off?" "Don't embarrass us," and "Joanne can do that better than you."

- Negative words beget negative actions.
- Negative words beget a poor self-image.
- Negative words beget low productivity.
- Negative words beget negative words!

We've all been with negative people who drag us down psychologically. When we stay around negative people, we lose hope. Negative people do not always verbalize their negative attitudes; they can influence other people in a negative way simply by not being positive.

Lack of praise is a negative. Children need to be praised. They need to be encouraged.

Many years ago a young boy struggled in school. His teacher called in his mother to give her the bad news that Ralph would probably never make it through high school, if he made it that far. His grandmother, hearing of the conversation, determined to encourage her grandson. Repeatedly she told him, "God has a special job for you to do. Study hard and be all He wants you to be." Ralph not only graduated from college but earned his master's degree.

We have a choice as parents—to focus on blessings and to encourage, or to focus on limitations and to discourage. Let's encourage our children, year by year and project by project.

When a child learns the satisfaction and feels the pride of accomplishing a goal, he is encouraged to tackle the next project.

PRAISE PRODUCES PRODUCTIVITY.
PRAISE PRODUCES SELF-CONFIDENCE.
PRAISE PRODUCES SECURITY.

PRAISE PRODUCES APPRECIATION.
PRAISE PRODUCES A DESIRE TO PLEASE!

When a teacher compliments your child, he will work harder to please that teacher. Mark Twain said, "I can live for a week on one good compliment." Compliments definitely motivate us and make us feel good about ourselves. Children need them often!

So much of raising a child involves discipline, which is like yucky medicine to cure an illness. I'm a strong believer in discipline, but I'm a stronger believer in preventive medicine. Praise is preventive medicine. Praise for good reinforces good and eliminates bad. The more we can praise for the good, the less we need to discipline for the bad.

> "Finally, brethren, whatever is true, whatever is honorable, whatever is right, whatever is pure, whatever is lovely, whatever is of good repute, if there is any excellence and if *anything worthy of praise, let your mind dwell on these things*" (Philippians 4:8).

Praise for Actions

> "Let us consider how to stimulate one another to love and good deeds" (Hebrews 10:24).

Children do not need to be the "best" to receive praise. They need to be doing *their* best. We live in a highly competitive society. There is a danger in being so competitive that you need to be the "best" or you do not want to participate in that activity. Children should be encouraged to do one or two things well (to develop their special gift or ability). Beyond that, they should have room to be average and have fun trying

lots of things. Balance is still the key. I'd rather have
a well-balanced child than a genius in one area who
is a misfit in society.

Sometimes developing children becomes *too* important to the parents. They push for only the "best." A
hockey team for seven- and eight-year olds can become
so sophisticated that the average good player is
excluded because "better" players are imported from
other divisions to make the best team. Let's let our kids
be kids. They need to do their best in school and excel
in "their" area. But let's allow them to do some things
just for fun, without getting caught up in competition.

Praise for Attitudes

Attitudes can be read like a thermometer. Children
need to be taught good attitudes. I have said that we
have frequently disciplined our children for a bad attitude. We also frequently praise them for a good attitude.

When a child has a positive attitude about work, we
praise her. When she has a good attitude after a hurtful
situation, we praise her. When she responds kindly
to a friend who has wronged her, we praise her. She
is learning about life. Life is not fair. Life sometimes
hurts. But if we can get over hurts and anger and
bitterness and respond in kindness, we will live more
peaceably. It is *bitterness* that hurts *us*—not the party
who wronged us.

Our family has chosen a passage of Scripture for our
family goal. For months it hung on the refrigerator
door. Now it sits on a page in our Family Counsel Notebook. Someday I hope to have it copied by a
calligrapher and hung on our kitchen wall as a
reminder of our chosen goal:

"Do nothing from selfishness or empty con-
ceit, but with humility of mind let each of

you regard one another as more important than himself; do not merely look out for your own personal interests, but also for the interests of others. Have this ATTITUDE in yourselves which was also in Christ Jesus" (Philippians 2:3-5).

Positive Praise and Pleasurable Parenting

Psychiatrists tell us it takes 20 positive strokes to make up for one negative slam. What's the scoreboard look like in most houses?

When we think about our child during the day, do we focus on the negative qualities that bug us, or do we rejoice in the positive qualities that make us want to hug our child and tell him how much we love him?

For 20 summers Dean and Chris have vacationed at Lake of the Woods, Canada, across the bay from my parents' summer home. For 20 summers we have observed Dean and Chris—as young marrieds, as parents of toddlers, as parents of teens. Each summer gave us a one-month glimpse into their family life, and over the years it has produced time-lapse photography, like a nature film that shows a beautiful flower in all its glory. If there is one trait that is evident with Dean and Chris, it's that they openly *love* their kids. They love being with them, they love doing things for them, they love working with them, and they love telling them how much they love them. Whether their kids were age three months, or three years, or 13 years, or 17 years, when we would ask "How are things going?" they would reply, "Great! We really enjoy our children." We enjoy their children too.

If the scoreboard in your household doesn't display a lot of sunshine, why not wipe the slate clean and start focusing 20-to-1 on the positives? Positive praise can produce pleasurable parenting for you too.

6

Beyond a Healthy Body

There are only two things that children share willingly—communicable diseases and their mother's age.

Communicable diseases are usually shared at Christmas or right before you leave on family vacation. Our 12-year-old was exposed to the usual childhood diseases many times, but apparently strong natural immunities prevented her from contracting any of them. When our youngest came down with chicken pox in June we didn't panic. She would be well by our July vacation. In mid-June our middle child broke out in red bumps. No problem. Two weeks later our 12-year-old broke out—competing to win the prize for the worst case ever. Never say never when rearing a child!

Surprise attacks of measles, chicken pox, colds, and the flu hit every family on the battlefield of child-rearing. We all survive these battles—a little scarred sometimes, but we survive.

"I can handle the battles. It's the *wars* I'm concerned about," preached my friend Karen. "The junk-food war, the no-exercise-sedate-generation war, the stress war, the child-abuse war, not to mention the drug war. The generation which our children has been born into has aimed its physical-abuse cannons right at their bodies."

I agree with Karen. Now, because of our dead and wounded, many parents are realizing that there has to be a better way. Nancy Reagan invests hours of her energy into advertising her antidrug convictions. Project Charlie groups around the country work to instill a proper self-image in the child as a defense against drugs and other physical abuse. Adults are waking up to the fact that they must change their unhealthy habits in an effort to save themselves and protect the next generation.

Many of our medical problems stem from lifestyle. Across the country hospitals are developing wellness programs in an effort to encourage people to be fitness-minded. Wellness may be the most positive medical step since the development of immunizations against the killer diseases. Wellness should be an enjoyable life pursuit. Lifestyle workshops are being offered by hospitals around the country to focus on weight-control, smoking cessation, stress-management, and good healthy living.

Let's examine some basic principles that we can build into the lives of our children.

Begin With a Healthy Body

1. *Natural foods for proper nutrition.*
"Can I have a candy bar, Mom?"

"Why not?" thought Betty. She had already let him have one that morning, and another wouldn't kill him. It was the only way to keep him quiet and out of her way.

At one time Betty was stricter about diet and nutrition. Then gradually one treat gave way to another, until now she has a junk-food addict on her hands.

Weaning him back to healthful, nutritious food will take some work.

A few years ago numerous health-and-nutrition books flooded the country. Mothers became aware of unhealthful preservatives, overprocessed foods, overcooked foods, and the danger of white sugar and white flour products. We learned that food affects our children's physical and emotional well-being. Many incorrect foods cause hyperactivity, misbehavior, depression, and even physical illnesses such as colds and ear infections.

I grew up with a mother who cooked three healthful, balanced meals a day. I learned about the "four food groups," but I never learned to like cooking. Some of my girlfriends *love* to cook. I don't. I relate to the mother who told her child she could pick out any box of cereal at the grocery store. She changed her mind when she saw the selection: "No, not that one! It has to be cooked!"

For the sake of my family's health (and our budget), I am cooking more now than I ever have before. I have read several health-food books. I am not a fanatic, but I am working toward a more nutritionally healthful lifestyle.

> "Whether then you eat or drink or whatever you do, do all to the glory of God" (1 Corinthians 10:31).

If you have questions in this area, consult with a nutritionist or your physician.

2. *Physical exercise.* Motherhood doesn't exactly enhance our figures (except when we're breastfeeding). Our stomachs have been stretched to colossal dimensions and our hips somehow fill out in sympathy to balance the look. After my first and second child

I lost the extra weight immediately and felt a little smug. Not so with my third! I am still exercising to get back in shape after delivering my third baby. (My "baby" is now seven years old!)

Exercise or physical activity must be an ongoing lifestyle. As much as I exercise to keep my body *looking* good, the primary goal is to keep my body *feeling* good. When should we begin teaching our child to exercise? Experts encourage us to begin at birth. Youngsters are usually active physically from natural drive and curiosity. Their "play" is often an athletic event.

As youngsters get older, balance is important. Athletes with natural ability will overemphasize exercise to the neglect of a balanced life in other areas. Nonathletic persons can become sedate and lazy and can start to look like blimps before they reach adolescence. Through walking, running, bike-riding, skating, swimming, gymnastics, tennis, or other sports, let's keep them exercising for their sake and for their health.

3. *Fresh air and sunshine.* Some forms of exercise take us to the great outdoors—a double dose of good health! When your infant is tiny, begin taking him for walks outdoors. Whether ten minutes in the stroller or an hour playing on a blanket in the park, you'll both benefit from the fresh air and sunshine.

4. *Water—the wonder drink.* Next to oxygen, water is the most important necessity for your body. Water is used in your digestion, circulation, absorption, and elimination. Just as water cleanses your exterior, water also cleanses your interior. So water those kids down!

Sufficient Sleep

"There never was a child so lovely but his mother was glad to get him asleep" (Ralph Waldo Emerson).

Sufficient sleep for a child not only keeps a child healthy and happy but keeps a young mother sane!

Carol and Bob were reminiscing about the days when their boys were young. "We loved those years—as busy as they were. But one nonnegotiable in our house was that our kids took naps until they started kindergarten."

Paul and I laughed in affirmation. We remembered our ground rules: During "quiet time" they were not allowed off their beds. Sometimes they were allowed to read or listen to a cassette tape. Usually they fell asleep.

In the evenings we put our children to bed at a set time so that we reserve some time as a couple to relax together. Both husband and wife have worked hard all day; both deserve to rest.

Both children and parents require adequate sleep each night. When mothers are overtired, overworked, overweight, and overextended they can hardly face getting dressed in the morning. They feel depressed, and the simplest task seems overwhelming. Children respond the same way we do. Healthy and rested, they're enjoyable. Overtired and not nutritionally fed, look out!

Children's sleeping schedules depend on their mother's routine. It is important to train children to sleep through the night. This requires more training with some children than others. They need to know when their bedtime is, and that once they are in bed, they may not get out. Schedules like this don't just happen by themselves. The couples who have their children in bed at a reasonable time each night and whose children stay in bed (excluding exceptions, such as illnesses and bad dreams) have accomplished this because they have taught their children in this area. They have established and maintained a regular routine.

Whatever your routine, be consistent. Start with a quiet-down period after the rigorous day of play. Bathe your child, do his teeth, take him potty, tuck him into bed, close closet doors, put on the night-light, make sure he has his teddy or blanky, read to him (if this is the time you do it), say prayers, kiss good-night, turn off the light, and walk out.

If he cries and you know you've met his needs, let him cry himself to sleep. He'll get the message eventually.

Meeting the needs of a helpless crying infant is virtuous. Being manipulated by a conniving toddler is vicious.

As our children grew older we often let them listen to a cassette tape recorder as they fell asleep. We chose quality Christian music with a positive message. Our children would fall asleep being reminded that they were very special and that God loved them very much.

Beyond a Healthy Body

Wellness represents a lifestyle beyond exercise and nutrition. It involves balance—in our physical, mental, emotional, and spiritual lives.

1. *The beauty of balance.* If athletic sports is your child's "thing," great! Then you need to balance out your child's life with an appreciation for things like art and music. If sports is not your child's "thing," then teach him or her to enjoy a few basic sports. Kent was obviously an artistic boy—gifted with creativity. His parents had a difficult time coaxing him outside to play with other youngsters. They decided to enroll him in the local soccer league. Cautious not to embarrass him by noticing his weak skills, they attended every game and cheered as he participated to the best of his ability.

After each game they would go out for pizza and enjoy some fun times with other families. Gradually Kent began to feel like "one of the guys." He knew he wasn't the star, and he still preferred his drawings to any soccer trophy he might stumble onto. But his participation enhanced his physical and social development.

The Cosby Show on TV has prompted many discussions in our family. Their versatility and balance is refreshing. Both parents are respected professionals and still enjoy the many facets of their home life and personal creativity. They have rediscovered the fun of creative family living. They know the balance between high standards in rearing their children and relaxed measures of freedom for hobbies and fun.

2. *Survival swimming.* Every child, athletic or not, should learn to swim. During our first 12 years of parenting we lived in California with a pool in our backyard. Learning to swim was a *matter of life and death.* As soon as our children could walk, we enrolled them in swim classes. We chose the method and the teacher by evaluating their results and how positive and loving their teaching was. Many six-month-olds are "drown-proofed" by competent instructors. Though we waited until our children were walking and talking, they were all good swimmers before they were two years old. They jumped off the board, floated, swam, and were totally relaxed in the water.

This proficiency doesn't mean that I allow them to swim unsupervised. Children should *always* be supervised near water. Don't let a phone call or a friend's visit distract you. SAFETY FIRST. Still, with proper swim instruction, if a child should accidently fall into a pool or lake, he will know how to swim to the side and pull himself out.

Swimming for survival becomes secondary after a child learns to love the water. The earlier you can expose your child to swimming, the better. Growing up in Canada, I spent my winters swimming at the YMCA and my summers in lakes. Colleagues of mine who were not around lakes as children had a difficult time overcoming their fear of water. It was difficult for them to enjoy this beautiful sport because they couldn't relax. So give your child the gift of safe swimming. Like riding a bike, once learned always remembered.

3. *Seasonable sports.* Every child needs to learn to ride a bike, roller-skate, ice skate (if you live in a cold climate), and play baseball, volleyball, and soccer. Your child need not excel in any sport, but he needs to participate in order to socialize in an athletic way, to learn the principles of good sportsmanship, and to balance out this area of his life.

If your child has opportunities to develop skills in water-skiing or snow-skiing or gymnastics or karate, encourage him. Whatever the sport, whatever the opportunity, open the door for your child to develop in this physical area of life.

Every child needs to also have a balanced view of sports and the opposite sex, realizing that either sex can win, depending on such factors as size and talent. If a girl beats a boy there shouldn't be any damage to the boy's ego any more than a girl should be damaged if a boy plays better.

The truth is that many boys will have a problem with this—especially boys who are small for their age. Mothers need to constantly affirm their children, focusing on everything positive they can point out so the youngster won't become angry or bitter or decide to "show the world" by turning into a bully or prodigal son. Physical inadequacies are difficult to overcome. Positive attitudes do make a difference.

"Short people try harder" is not a positive attitude

or proper motivation. Each person needs the freedom to accept who he is without extra pressures put on him by a competitive peer group. Gordie is one of the neatest guys I've ever met. He's very short for a male— inches shorter than I am—but I feel so good around him because he feels so good about himself. As a mother, let your child know how much you love and accept him.

The Real Reasons

Why do you jog? Why does your son play soccer? Why does your daughter take gymnastics?

If we are motivated by desire for a healthy body and well-balanced child, wonderful! If we are motivated to develop the natural ability or talent our child possesses—great! However, many parents are not as pure in their purposes.

1. *Motivated to win.* According to Dr. Jerome Vogel, Medical Director at the New York Institute for Child Development, there are negative results of too much competition at too early an age. One of them is that children get badly damaged egos.

"Do your best" is the best motivation we can instill in our child. A child's best can and will improve as he practices. The word "best" needs to be followed by a word of caution: If we honestly want our child to perform the best he can and we can honestly accept that, then we will praise him even if his best happens to be the worst on his team. But if our definition of "best" really means he is expected to win, we have put unfair pressure on our child. This shows that we care more about image than we do about qualities of our child such as good sportsmanship.

Good sportsmanship in losing is worthy of praise! Two necessary goals in sports are to have fun and to gain skills. A child doesn't need to win in order to accomplish these goals.

2. *Motivated to show off.* Many people choose a sport because they enjoy the activity, the exercise, and the challenge. Many others are attracted by the glamorous equipment and the high cost to participate. They turn the activity into an "elitist" sport. The sport is not wrong, but the attitude could be.

If our reason for taking up water-skiing or boating is because no one else in our neighborhood can afford anything but a paddleboat, our motivation is wrong. As our child excels in this sport, he also excels in his haughty attitude. This does not need to happen. Our daughters love to water-ski. They know they are fortunate to spend one month each year at "Seven C's," their Grandpa and Grandma Corbett's summer home on Lake of the Woods, Ontario. This is an annual family reunion where my four sisters and I, along with our children, meet to enjoy a vacation and reaffirm our relationship. We realize that this is a special privilege. Not every family is so fortunate.

Yours might be a family that plans an elaborate family reunion. Or you might be a family that has yet to explore the possibility of this kind of extended bonding. Perhaps your family boasts a ski lodge or an ocean-side villa. Or you might be a family that boasts a pup tent and hibachi. What we have is not as important as our attitude and our motivation for what we do.

If your family snow-skis together, teach your kids an attitude of appreciation rather than superiority. Or maybe you have sons who play hockey. Is their equipment valued because they take care of their things, or is it valued as something to show off? Mothers who have outfitted a child through garage-sale buys, hand-me-downs, and leftovers are aware of the importance of sport for the sport's sake. The purpose of sports is not to compare material possessions.

I laugh when I think about the cartoon in which two mothers are jogging down the lane in their gorgeous sweat suits, matching tennis shoes, and coordinated headbands. A man is jogging past them, clad in an old gray sweatshirt, torn shorts, sneakers that look like they toughed high school with him, and sweat pouring from his brow. One of the sweet-smelling mothers comments to the other, "How disgusting! People shouldn't participate in a sport if they can't afford it!"

3. *Motivated to have my child fulfill my unachieved dreams.* Secretly Marvis has never gotten over the fact that she never made senior cheerleader at her high school. Outwardly she says she was too busy to do that, but inside she was devastated. Secretly she vowed that if she had a daughter, she would work with her and make sure she made it. Now she has a teenage daughter, but the daughter doesn't want to be a cheerleader. Marvis pushes her and manipulates her—"for her child's own good," she says.

Dads are no better; they want a football star. "Think of the bucks it would save us if this kid got a scholarship," they rationalize. That's true, *if* this is what the child wants. But if this is just the father's abilities, dreams, desires, and drives but not the son's—look out!

> "Train up a child in the way he should go, and even when he is old he will not depart from it" (Proverbs 22:6).

"In the way he should go" should cause us to—

- Get to know our child as a "one of a kind," unique person.
- Discover what our child's abilities and aptitudes are.

- Help us focus on developing him as a person with a special purpose (rather than pushing him to go the way we wish we had gone).
- Set goals with our child.
- Study Scripture to determine what God says about how our child should go (character-building).
- Focus on balanced training for our child, involving the physical, mental, emotional, social, and spiritual paths of life.

We need to ask ourselves, "Who is the ultimate person I want my child to please?" It should not be ourselves or our husband or the grandparents or the teachers or the coaches. It should be God.

Sports is one area where we can praise and encourage our child, but not the only area. Too many parents are like Ben, who waved his finger at his son and said, "You look disgraceful. Your hair and clothes embarrass me. I'm ashamed of your grades. I hate to admit you're a member of our family." Later that same day on the soccer field, his son scored a goal. "Way to go, Son!" he yelled, "That's MY BOY!"

Healthful Family Activities

In our jet-age society, with executive demands on our time, it's often difficult to justify leisure activities, especially with the family. A golf game with the corporation bigwigs is an acceptable alternative for exercise. Tennis with the swingers at the club at least elevates us socially. But what about our priorities? Each family member needs recreation to counteract the stress in our lives.

Why not take time to walk together as a family?

Since our children were infants we have enjoyed walking around the blocks together, "cruising" the neighborhood, getting caught up on each other's day. Since we've moved to Edina (Minneapolis), we walk around the many lakes in our area! It's more than "a breath of fresh air"; the scenery is magnificent and the family sharing even better.

Or, as a family, try bike-riding. We've come through 12 years of the youngest one riding in an infant carrier on the back of Mommy or Daddy's bike. Finally we can all ride together. Sometimes a half-hour ride in the evening is all we can fit in. Sometimes we set aside a Saturday morning to ride to a park, where we enjoy a thermos of coffee or hot chocolate with fresh muffins or sweet rolls. A picnic breakfast with the family lets them know how much we value being together.

Activities to Tire Out the Kids

I admit, I have ulterior motives! Especially with younger children, heavy physical activity during the day will tire them out. They'll be ready to go to bed earlier and will fall asleep faster, leaving a quiet evening for you and your husband. Don't feel guilty about it. Children need physical activity and they need sound sleep.

I've told you about our summer vacations at the lake. My sisters and I know the value of lots of swimming, running, hiking, canoeing, sailing, sun, fresh air, hearty dinners, and early bedtime! It gives us many evenings for adult visiting and time off from motherhood responsibilities.

Respecting and Protecting Their Bodies

Don't you wish such words as "incest," and "child sexual abuse" didn't exist? Why do we have to subject our innocent, naive children to the information about the possible dangers awaiting them? It's a sick society we live in, a dangerous society. If there's any way I can prevent my child from being a victim, I want to. Here are some suggestions.

1. *Protect your youngster as much as possible.* Accept 24-hour-a-day responsibility for your preschooler. Know where he is and what he's doing at all times. At a restaurant or public place, do not allow him to go to a restroom alone. Sometimes this inconvenience takes energy and forethought. The difficulty usually arises when a son gets too old to go into the women's restroom with Mom, or when Dad is out with his daughter. If a child needs to go into a restroom without you, assure him that you'll stand just outside the restroom door until he comes out. Tell your child you will not move, and then don't. If he should need you, he should just call you. If a minor problem arises, you can send in another man. If you think he is in real trouble, it takes you two seconds to march right in there. If your child goes into a large restroom, you might crack the door open a bit while your child is in there.

Admittedly, there is the risk of embarrassment. Tom tells of the evening he took his four-year-old daughter out for a pizza date. He was standing outside the door of the ladies' restroom when he heard Heather call for him. In he marched, only to find a distressed daughter trying to get her clothes back on. He quickly helped her and was about to exit when another woman walked in. He mumbled something, trying to explain, as she huffed and squealed and squawked. But had a real threat endangered his child, Tom would have been there to protect her.

When should a mother allow her son to use a men's restroom? Depending on the child, age four, five, or six, or when *he* begins to question you or feel embarrassed with you. Then have Dad rehearse with him the "how-to's" in a men's public restroom, so he's trained for when he's out with you.

In providing 24-hour-a-day protection for your youngster, carefully choose your babysitters. Char used to hire different sitters as an "outreach" until she learned that her children had watched disgusting TV shows and had added to their vocabulary while Dad and Mom were gone. When these four-letter words began to pop out, Char decided to choose her babysitters more carefully and share the Lord in a way that wouldn't put her children in jeopardy.

Because the babysitters have a great responsibility, I only hire reputable Christian girls whom I know quite well.

Now that our older daughters are babysitting, we still feel a responsibility for their safety. We like to meet the parents who hire them, whether we go to their home or they come to ours, and we note the address and phone number and approximate hours they will be gone.

If your child needs to stay at a child care facility or a friend's home, evaluate the care and influence that will affect your child. By making responsible decisions, 90 percent of possible danger can be avoided.

2. *Teach your child to protect his own body.* You quite naturally teach your child not to run out in front of a car on the street. You teach your toddler to play catch with a ball, not a glass. Remember to teach your child to protect himself against all dangers—including strangers. You might be worried that your children will become afraid of all people. They're not afraid to ride in your car or to wash your car. They have *learned* to be afraid of running out in front of a car. They're not afraid to have a glass of water or juice. They have

learned to be afraid to throw the glass or hear the dangerous sound of smashing glass.

Teach children the *danger* of people who might want to steal them or hurt them. Teach them to run away from strangers who might try to bribe them. Rehearse these rules: "Don't talk to strangers. Don't accept rides from strangers. Don't accept candy from strangers." Role-play their response to dangerous situations such as:

> A man says he lost his dog. He shows you a picture of the dog. He has tears in his eyes and asks you to help him find his dog.
> A man says your dad or mom has been hurt in an accident and the police asked him to come to pick you up and take you to the hospital to be with your dad or mom.
> A woman says she'll give you a hundred dollars if you go with her and help her do something. She shows you the hundred dollars and says how surprised and happy your dad and mom will be when you come home with that money.

For each situation ask, "What would you do?" Discuss what is right and what is wrong.

3. *Teach your child to respect his body.* Now comes the more difficult task. A child does not need to know the details of child abuse, but he needs to know enough so that he knows when he is in danger.

A good friend of mine, Lynn Heitritter, has written a workbook entitled *Little Ones* which teaches children to respect and protect their bodies. This is a good tool. Do not be embarrassed to discuss this important matter with your child. Let me stress again that children don't need gross details; adults can barely handle hearing this information. Children *do* need to know for certain what is right and what is wrong.

One way to illustrate this is to discuss with them why they wear a bathing suit. Explain that a bathing suit covers their *private parts*. Reinforce that everyone, no matter how young or how old, is entitled to keep their private parts private. How will they know if someone has done something wrong? Because that person probably touched or looked at a part of their body that should be covered by their bathing suit. It's that simple.

Children should not be made "paranoid" about hugs and love pats from friends and relatives. But children should also realize that even a close friend or relative *could* do something wrong. Each child needs to know what is right and what is wrong.

Another potential problem is that children might not be touched, but might be looked at or photographed in a wrong way.

Role-play the following situation to warn your child:

> A man comes to our door while Mommy and Daddy are not home. You recognize him as a friend of the family, so you let him in. He tells you he is a photographer and he wants to take some pictures so he can surprise your parents. He makes you promise never to tell anyone so you won't ruin the surprise. Then he tells you to take off your clothes, like you do for the doctor. You feel a little funny, but he seems nice and he convinces you that he has permission to do this and that you will get a reward if you cooperate and do what you are told.

Now ask these questions: "What would you do?" "What is right?" "What is wrong?" Children need to know that no matter who, what, where, when, or why—they *never* need to do *anything* if they believe that *it is wrong*.

Finally, keep all lines of communications open, no matter what. Our children should feel free to tell us anything, ask any questions, or discuss any topic with us. We're contemporary women. Let's not be shocked or overreact. We can handle it. Our child needs to know, and we want to be the one to give him or her the correct information.

Discovering and Sharing the Facts of Life

In sharing with hundreds of women, I have discovered that very few learned the facts of life from their parents. They heard it (in detail and with immoral overtones) from their peers. That's right—*they learned it on the streets*. The information may or may not have been accurate. We're talking about wonderful Christian families who taught their children Scripture but not the practical facts of life. Many young girls were never even taught about menstruation. The day they began their period they thought something terrible had happened to them and they were going to die. How uncivilized for mothers to think that by not discussing a problem it will go away! How cowardly of mothers to hope that their child somehow finds out about sex so they never get asked to explain it to them!

If we as mothers do not want to teach our child about sex, who do you wish to take our place? A physician? Rarely do mothers take their child to a physician for a physical explanation. Besides, children rarely require all the information at one time. They ask and digest little by little. Some months they're inquisitive and receptive, some months they're not.

Would we rather have a teacher or secular counselor

educate our child? Public school sex education will have no moral or biblical foundation. For many children, this is the only correct biological information they will hear. For Christian families, this might force the discussion at home as parents seek to give the Christian perspective that was missing in the school presentation. At school they will not gain the vision of sexual intercourse as a beautiful expression of love *within* their future marriage. Parents need to reinforce the purpose of their children protecting their bodies until they marry, and for girls, looking forward to the day when their bodies will produce children.

If your child has learned about sex from his peers, you can count on having some correcting to do.

If your child is in the fourth, fifth, or sixth grade and you haven't had "a little talk" yet, you're probably already at the correcting stage. Don't give up. Tackle it in love.

Teaching my own daughters about this delicate subject is a privilege and a challenge. Paul and I answer little questions as they arise. We're very open and natural about our bodies. The girls showered with Paul or me until they were kindergarten age. As they grew older we covered up more, but we don't gasp if they accidentally walk into our room and we're not dressed. There's a fine line between being relaxed with our bodies and maintaining a healthy respect between the generations. Respect is the key element. We don't joke about nudity.

A natural acceptance of our bodies should never be confused with modesty and decency or with child sexual abuse, as discussed in the previous section. Children are curious, and if you answer their questions when they first ask them, *you* will be the one who will get to teach them what you want them to know about this exciting subject!

When our children were young, we used non-threatening books about animals to begin to teach the facts of life. We began with "How Puppies Are Born." We moved from puppy books to people books. The first books were cartoon in nature and told how babies grew and were born (but not how they got into the mommy's tummy). The next books we used showed scientific diagrams and used proper names to describe the basic simple facts. We used our local library to supply us with what we needed at the time.

One excellent text is *Marvelous Me* by Dr. Anne Townsend. It's designed to help young people learn more about their bodies, addressing topics such as heart, lungs, kidneys, bones, muscles, skin, nerves, brains, nutrition, and the basics of sex.

I'll never forget our first "big" talk. Melanie had asked the right questions, so I told her I would find a good book to show her and we would discuss it on Saturday morning. When the morning arrived, Paul and I poured ourselves a cup of coffee, took Melanie in the living room alone, closed the doors behind us, and sat down on the couch together. Melanie giggled as she sat between us. The book was basic—Paul read it, then prayed, then asked if she had any questions. Your husband may not feel free to do this, but Paul wanted to be close to his girls and he wants them to feel free to come to him at any time to discuss any subject.

If you have a son, you will probably feel more comfortable with a "father-son" talk between your husband and your son. You might suggest it and set up the time or the outing when you feel your son has reached that stage of curiosity. You should share with your husband what information you hope he'll cover. Perhaps you could go to the bookstore or library and get him a book for an aid.

If your son comes to you with specific questions, be open and honest, respectfully giving him the information he requests. "Teachable moments" involve seizing an opportunity when a child is obviously curious, and using this time to teach the facts of life and right from wrong. Don't give more information than the child can handle at his age. But do complete your sex education just before your child reaches puberty, since after this point he is usually embarrassed by discussions of sex with his parents.

Children and Television Abuse

Inside most homes lurks a potential child-abuser— the television set. Immorality is glamorized in many television shows. Violence is an exciting part of living. According to research at the University of Illinois, children who watch violence on television are more likely to commit violent crimes when they become adults.

We as parents need to protect our children's minds from the garbage ready to invade them. Censor what they watch. Control how much they watch. Encourage attentive educational programs. And when it is sunny outside, have them play outside.

Children start school these days with a big advantage: They already know two letters of the alphabet— TV! We allowed our youngsters to watch the usual Sesame Street-type programs, which reinforced their alphabet and reading skills. On Saturdays they could watch some cartoons. As the children grew and their responsibilities grew, we limited their TV to one hour a day. Recently, with more homework and piano practice, we allow only one-half hour a day per child. This may sound severe when compared with the national averages, but we are also aware that some cultured families choose to not own a television set at all.

Remember, children who watch television every night will go down in history—not to mention arithmetic, geography, and science!

If you happen to own a VCR, use it to your advantage. We have ruled that the half-hour of television can't be watched until music practice is done and homework is completed. The immediate complaint is "But my very favorite show is on at seven and I could never finish everything by then." We've countered by buying each child a blank video cassette and printing her name on it. Our response to the complaint is, "We will record what you want to see and you may watch it after your work is completed."

Of course there are exceptions to the rule. And anytime the *family* decides to watch a show together, the rule is overlooked for that night.

Fun and Healthy Laughter

Dave and Eunie enjoy the funny side of life. Their boys will grow up and remember the good times—rolling on the floor laughing together.

One time my parents were visiting us from Canada, and Eunie invited us all to dinner. When we pulled up in front of the house and saw her sons' bikes and toys and balls scattered across the lawn and walkway, I was surprised because Eunie is meticulously neat. When we saw the front door smeared with mud I thought, "She must have had a busy day with her three little guys." When Dave and Eunie answered the door in their pajamas and housecoat, shocked looks on their faces, I suspected something was up. As we were seated in their beautiful living room, I noticed lampshades tilted, pictures crooked, and ornaments amiss. Over in the corner sat a garbage can. By this time I was getting a little embarrassed for my respectable parents.

As we were led into the dining room for dinner, we noticed that the table service was not the elegant china table setting that Eunie usually uses. We had soup ladles, tongs, and carving knives for silverware, jars for cups, and an assortment of lids and trays for plates. From a mystery menu we had to choose the order in which our courses would be served: We had mints first, then some peas, then a piece of pie, then a chicken dish. By now we were howling with laughter! The evening held several more surprises, but we weren't surprised when Dave and Eunie ended with a "HAPPY APRIL FOOLS' DAY" to all of us. We will always remember that April first!

My husband enjoys humor. If things are a little dull around our house, he'll tickle our minds. Leaving for work one morning, he called the kids to the front door to kiss him goodbye. "Daddy, Daddy," they squealed, "you forgot something!" There he stood in his best sports jacket with shirt and tie, hair well-groomed, briefcase in hand, shoes polished—but no slacks! Just his undershorts. They laughed about that one for a long time.

> "A joyful heart is good medicine" (Proverbs 17:22).

There is a healing power in laughter. In ancient times, royal courts were often enlivened by the antics of a professional fool. Like King Solomon of old, those crowned heads—so often weighted down with the burdens of state—knew that "laughter is a good medicine." They valued the presence of a jester.

Today philosophers and doctors have found that laughter counteracts the physiological effects of stress. A laugh at just the right time can bring healing relief, even in the midst of crisis or distress. With siblings, laughter tends to defuse feelings of anger or vengeance. A joking comment or silly face can soothe tempers, cleanse the air during an argument, or reestablish rapport after correction.

Remembering the seeds we have planted and the importance of all we're teaching in our homes, let's cultivate a sense of humor!

7

Straight A's or You're Grounded

Child prodigies are children with highly imaginative parents.

Admittedly, we mothers are amazed at the remarkable capabilities of our offspring. When we enroll them in kindergarten we're sure they will be the star of the class and the gleam in the teacher's eye.

Unfortunately, some become the tear in the teacher's eye. Some mothers are so ashamed of their unruly child that they wish they could attend PTA meetings under an assumed name.

Tony Campolo compares Jewish families with other American families in their attitude toward education. The Jewish mother calls to her child as he leaves for school, "Do you have your books?" The American mother calls out to her child, "Do you have your lunch?"

Zig Ziglar sympathizes with parents who think that to raise kids successfully they need the genius of an Einstein, the insight of a psychologist, the stamina of a distance runner, the humor of Bob Hope, the faith of Daniel in the lions' den, and the courage of David as he faced Goliath! He encourages us to take heart because there are no perfect parents, and we aren't going to be the first.

Desiring the best for our child is admirable. Determining what the best is for our child is difficult! Desiring to properly motivate our child is admirable. Determining what that proper motivation is can be very difficult. Desiring straight A's from a child with below-average mental ability is an injustice. We as parents need a clearer understanding of what is realistic for our child's capabilities.

As mothers we are informed about our child's shoe size and shirt size. We keep track of his dental and medical records and his immunization shots, and we schedule periodic checkups. But we rarely give even equal attention to an area more important than the physical—the mental health and development of our child.

> "As he [your child] thinks within himself, so he is" (Proverbs 23:7).

This encompasses his self-esteem, but also his reasoning and thinking styles. How does your child think? What are you doing to develop and guide his thinking? Let's consider our child's *formal education* and *informal education*, then look at an area where many of us feel a lack—*common sense*.

Formal Education for Your Child

A mother's goals used to be to get her child into school so the teacher could teach the basics—readin', 'ritin', and 'rithmetic. As motherhood became a competitive sport, some women began pushing their children into preschool reading and developing other visible skills that would increase her sense of value as a mother. Preschoolers *are* capable learners, but they are also necessary "players." Balance between teaching and play is necessary. Childhood is a once-in-a-lifetime experience—not to be lost and not to be relived. Children need time for creative play and time for fun for the sake of having fun. Many preschool children do have the mental ability to begin developing skills essential to their ultimate success in life. As they are able and interested, begin to focus on three key areas: language, reading, and memory.

1. *Language.* "Please pass de besketti" (spaghetti). "I sure like hangabers" (hamburgers). "These meetdolls (meatballs) taste yukky." "Are we going to the store possit (post office) today?" Baby talk is so much fun—for Daddy and Mommy and any other audience present. We like to think, "We could take this kid on the road! He'd be a hit!"

Parents are so proud when their child graduates past the crying stage, the cooing stage, and the babbling stage—first words, then phrases, then sentences. Sheer genius.

Language is a natural. What mother doesn't enjoy talking? And what child, when he learns to speak, ever wants to keep quiet?

We can begin teaching our child to talk at birth. Talk directly to your infant, face to face, eyeball to eyeball, expressing information and love in a positive way. Infants *can* be stimulated mentally when we converse intelligently with them. Let this be our pattern for life.

It's important to speak proper English so our child will hear and learn proper English. Use proper terms for physical parts of the body. Be dignified and respectful when addressing your children. Be polite in addressing one another. Show respect verbally and your child will learn these important language skills by rote.

Language comes quite naturally for most children.

If your child has a problem with speech, seek professional counsel and practice the therapy that is suggested. But don't panic about your child's verbal future. Most children catch up with their peers before they finish elementary school. Occasionally, speech difficulties may cause you to discover a learning problem, mental retardation, a physical problem, or an anxiety problem with your child. That's why it's so important to continually seek to know your child so you can best determine what help he needs in his mental development.

Caution: Children *do* repeat what they hear at home and *do* cause us embarrassment as they reveal "classified information" at inopportune times.

Children seldom misquote you; they repeat word for word what you shouldn't have said in the first place.

If you have not reached this stage of motherhood, your days are numbered!

Over the years our "darling daughters" have informed our congregations, friends, and even total strangers of the secret details of our daily lives. In case you haven't heard, I got a speeding ticket while driving to Yohns for coffee. And yes, Paul and I occasionally soak in the bath together. Yes, Daddy tried smoking when he was a boy and he got in big trouble.

Language can be a lethal weapon. You need to explain to your children over and over that some things are private family business and should *never* be discussed outside the family.

We try to live honestly before our children so they don't feel they're covering up for hypocrisy. We explain that private family business includes:

- How much things cost (houses, furniture, gifts, etc.).
- How much we weigh.

- When one of the siblings has gotten into trouble and been disciplined.
- When Daddy and Mommy have had a "big discussion."
- When an older sister has a crush on a certain boy.
- When we are planning a surprise party or gift for someone.

I'm sure you'll want to add to your list.

We've also had to teach them what is not appropriate to ask other people. That may be harder to anticipate. Deanna was introduced to Denice's fiance, and as quickly as her little mind could think she blurted out, "How many children are you going to have?"

Children can also come to amazing conclusions without any valid input from us. When we first arrived at our new church in Edina, I had to unpack and get the girls settled in school. With Paul busy in his new ministry, I purposed to stay home for awhile in an effort to smooth out the family's adjustment from California to Minnesota. We didn't discuss any of this in front of the kids. On our first Sunday at church, our seven-year-old announced to her teacher, "My mom usually plays the piano and sings and teaches and speaks. But she's going to kick back here."

Considering the dangers ahead, maybe you're not so anxious to develop your child's language skills!

2. *Reading.*

Read to your children as often as you can. At one-and-a-half years old Kyle could be found lying in his room, flat on his back with his legs crossed, "reading" a book. You'd almost believe it was for real because, having heard the stories over and over, he repeated the correct words by the pictures on each page. Randy and Darlene have read to Kyle and their other children since they were tiny, developing in them a love for reading.

Let your children see you reading. My children often see me curled up on our couch with a bowl of popcorn—reading, not watching TV. Each night Paul and I usually get into bed and read before we go to sleep. We have extra-fluffy pillows with good reading lamps on each side. We have provided the same for our children: a bedside lamp, bright enough for reading, and two pillows for each bed so they can comfortably prop themselves up. We encourage them to follow our model, and enjoy this quiet time before they sleep.

Let your children read aloud to you. During kindergarten and first grade your child will be required to read aloud. Usually your child's teacher will send home primary readers for your child to read to you. Continue this practice as they grow older. It helps develop their reading skills and their oral presentation skills.

Have books available in your home. As I decorate and arrange each room in my home, I always ask myself, "What is the purpose for this room? What is the focal point of this room?" When the primary purpose is *conversation* or *relaxation* I group my furniture to form a conversation area. If my purpose is reading, I make sure there are good reading lamps. In the family room and the children's bedrooms I have shelves for books. Having lots of books available encourages reading in our home.

Visit your library together. Darlene and her preschool daughter, Tara, made a special trip to the library to find the answer to a very important question that Tara was asking: Does a fly have a brain? A librarian helped them find the information. Tara learned that a fly does have a brain, and even saw what it looked like.

Many libraries provide a free story-hour for preschool children. As your children become older they will need to understand the library system in order to research projects for school assignments. Begin teaching this when they are young. When they ask a question and you don't have the answer, show them how they can find the answers.

Schedule a reading time each day. Before a child begins school, daily expose your child to the world of books. Try to schedule time each day to read to him, then provide him a quiet time to read alone. Forming good habits now will benefit your child for a lifetime.

Recognize the value of reading. Reading is a gift you can give your child that represents money, status, experience, and culture—because you are enriching his or her life through books. Mothers who raise children in low economic or culturally difficult circumstances can lift their children out of that setting by allowing them to benefit from the experiences they read about. Not only will your child be stimulated mentally and therefore achieve in school, but he will also understand more of the possibilities of this life and the potential that is within him.

As soon as our children began to read, we bought them their first Bible and inscribed: "As you are learning to read, we want you to have your own Bible. We pray that you will learn to read this most important book—God's Word—every day. May you become grounded in the real truths and standards that God has designed for you.

With love, Dad and Mom."

3. *Memory.* In this age of computers and high technology, we more fully value and appreciate the capabilities of a human mind. If your family is frantically saving for a home computer, realize the equity you already possess in the *minds* of you and your children.

Memory is a key to spelling, arithmetic, science, and

history. It is also essential to our spiritual growth.

Have you ever sat in church and watched children quote entire chapters of Scripture, then thought, "How can they do that?" Even more startling is the realization that *our* children are just as capable. It's the old rule of nature: What goes in comes out. Stop and evaluate if your children can only recite 15 television commercials.

By my children's second birthday they could correctly quote John 3:16. I acknowledge that they were accelerated *verbally*, but otherwise they're average, normal kids. It's just that I had *taught* them the verse. Children probably memorize easier at that young age than we do today as adults. We should never underestimate our child's ability and possibilities.

By age 3½ our daughters knew all the books of the Bible. When my mom was 3½ years old her mother taught her the books of the Bible set to a simple tune. When I was 3½ my mother taught them to me and I performed them on the Children's Back-to-the-Bible Radio Broadcast (the height of my career!). I taught them to each of my girls by age 3½, and they performed them in family concerts at various churches across the country. Our kids aren't smarter than yours. Most children are capable of memorizing *what we teach them*! Let's enjoy the challenge.

Choosing a School for Your Child

There are many options available today:

- The public school in our community.
- A specialty school (magnet school) that provides enrichment in arts, sciences, or sports. (This school could be miles away and require an interdistrict transfer.)

- A private school.
- A Christian private school.
- Home schooling.
- Preschools, nurseries, Montessori schools.

In determining God's will or at least God's direction in choosing the school for our child, we need to take time to know our child's needs and learn the benefits of each option. The local public school is our easiest option and may or may not be the best choice. Before your child reaches kindergarten age, visit the school, sit in on some sessions, and discuss the school's philosophy with the teacher or principal.

Cliff Schimmels adds much light to the subject in *How to Help Your Child Survive and Thrive in Public School*. This Christian educator stresses the importance of the teacher, and how necessary it is for you as a parent to evaluate and select the environment conducive to your child's learning. That's why it's so important to know your child's personality and particular learning needs.

If you are considering a specialty school, call your local school district and ask them to send you information on what their schools offer. If one appeals to you, visit the school first.

If you are considering a private school, visit the school and interview the principal. You are in effect hiring the school to educate your child, so you want to feel satisfied with your purchase. Even if you choose to send your child to a nonpublic school and make the financial sacrifices needed to keep him there, remember that you are still responsible for your child's growth. You may be paying double taxes for schooling, but you are still the most important educational agent in your child's life.

If you feel strongly about educating your child in a

Christian environment, investigate before you register. Not *all* Christian schools teach Christian principles as you might understand them. Ask for a copy of the school's statement of faith. Discuss teaching philosophy plus any issues that might bother you. Not *all* Christian schools provide an overall quality education. Ask if the school is certified, and with what agency. What are the qualifications of the teachers? What type of music or sports programs do they offer? Examine the facilities they use.

If your child continues in a Christian school through high school, find out if they have a band and football team as well as home ec and shop classes. Know what you are paying for.

In recent years home schooling has become a popular option for dedicated mothers. The basic concept from Deuteronomy 6:7 encompasses all facets of education until the parents feel the child should transfer into a formal school setting.

This growing movement is documented in *Home Schools*, by Cheryl Gordon. Figures from the National Association for the Legal Support of Alternative Schools shows that home-schooling families grew from a few thousand in 1976 to 75,000 in 1984.

I am a dedicated parent, but I still feel a pang of disbelief when I encounter a home-school mother who is accepting total responsibility for her child's mental development. I realize that many mothers have done this for years, and I commend them, but let me be honest about my apprehensions.

I taught in a public elementary school for four years before I began my family. I loved teaching, but it was a challenging, full-time career. I worked at it eight, ten, twelve hours a day. My education and student-teaching were in this field. And still I felt inadequate in certain subject areas—especially science, new math, and now computers. As a parent I don't believe I could give my child all that she is receiving at her school (even my first-grader). I don't even own a computer.

Second, I taught piano for 17 years. I regularly pleaded with my mothers to spend a half-hour a day helping their child practice. Mothers promised and planned and were enthusiastic, but rarely did it happen. As a mother, I try to help each of my children with a half-hour to an hour of piano practice each day. The older ones do more on their own. Sometimes I'm consistent, sometimes I'm not. I consider myself a fairly structured, disciplined person. My concern is this: If most mothers can't sit and work with a child one hour a day, how do they *realistically* plan to teach them all subjects?

I am not against home schooling but I am challenging you to deeply consider whether you as a mother are best suited for home schooling. If so, how and for how long? There are many books available to help you and support groups to encourage you and keep you on track.

Many mothers choose to enroll their preschoolers in a couple-of-mornings-a-week enrichment class or social activity group. This broadens the child's world and gives Mother some time for herself. I personally chose to keep my children home with me until the day they started kindergarten. I loved these days of working and playing together. Melanie and Cheryl were 19 months apart, so I had five busy years at home. Deanna, in contrast, had five years home alone with me after Melanie and Cheryl began school. When Deanna was 3½ years old, I began a business and continued my career as a musician. I chose to keep Deanna with me. She played by my side. We stopped regularly for hug breaks. We only worked till one P.M. each day, then went home for naptime before the other girls arrived home from school.

You need to determine—in your setting and within your budget—what is best for you. Each child is unique and custom-made, and you as a mother can watch your plant bloom as you choose appropriate soil and provide water and sunshine for it.

Be Involved in Their Education

As a mother, I have volunteered my services at my children's school for the past eight years. I spend an hour or two a week helping, usually in the field of music, since this is my area of greatest strength. I have personally benefited because through my participation I understand better my children's school environment. I understand better my children's ability to learn, to socialize, to obey rules, to respond to authority, and to cope with another area of life. And I also understand how to pray for my children, their teachers, and their schoolmates.

My children have also benefited because they and their teachers see what a high priority I put on my children's education. As I work with the teachers and visit with them during coffee breaks, they get to know and understand me, which helps them know and understand my children better.

Remember that the teacher can only teach and motivate so far. Much of your child's educational success depends on your child. As he gets older, use the following to help him reach his goals.

What and why. Sit down and discuss educational goals and reasons. Write out these guidelines.

When. Plan a specific time each day for study, homework, reading, and practice. We use schedules at our house to prove to our children that study is possible.

Where. Provide a place for your child to study. If you can buy a desk and a good light for his room, do. We painted old desks for our children when they were young. Many nights they preferred working at the kitchen table. Wherever, the rule was that the house should be quiet (within reason) during this study time.

How. In every area, encourage your child. Praise him for achievements. Help with assignments—driving him to the library, helping him assemble science projects. This not only raises his grades but inspires him to dream bigger dreams and tackle higher goals.

Motivate for the Future

While our children were in the primary grades we began dreaming out loud about what colleges they might attend. Those years are still ahead of us, but the girls have caught our vision and are already excited about continuing their education.

Your child may be suited for university, or college, or Bible college, or a vocational school, or a trade school, or something else. Not every child must go to college; it depends on his calling. As you seek to know your child better, help him to discover his likes and abilities. Help him to get excited about his eventual life's work. Plan, pray, and save together for your child's future education.

I don't know about you, but the cost of putting three children through college overwhelms me. If I thought about it long enough I'd start to cry. Praying is definitely the best option. I've been praying that my children would be so brilliant or talented or athletic that they would receive full scholarships through college. However, that's pretty unrealistic. Another prayer has been that a relative would leave an inheritance to provide for my children's college. That's about as likely as the full scholarship! Besides, who would want even a distant relative to have to die for the cause? Through further prayer, I have begun to realize that God has given me the ability to plan, at least in part. Setting aside a little money each month can be at least a start in providing college for our girls. If that's not enough, I can pray that God will meet the rest.

Model for your child the fact that life itself is an education. Hopefully you are continuing to learn.

Informal Education for Your Child

Our senior pastor has known our family since prechildren days. We watched Rick and Linda raise their boys for a number of years before we began our own family. They in turn have watched us parent our three children during the past 14 years. Rick has always stressed that we need to use "teachable moments" in educating our children. Daily living is a 24-hour classroom. These teachable moments have proved to be very interesting.

One evening shortly after Cheryl was born, Paul and Rick looked after the four children while Linda and I went out. When Cheryl messed her diaper Rick casually called Steven, his eight-year-old son, to come and observe as Paul changed the diaper. He casually explained to Steven that girls are different from boys, and then asked if Steven was noticing that fact. Steven replied, "Yeah, girls stink!" Some teachable moments are more productive than others!

If you watch for teachable moments, I guarantee that your life will be enriched with greater knowledge, understanding, and humor!

Common Sense: Caught and Taught

Dan, Erna, Paul and I have spent hours debating the

topic of common sense. We agree that it's worth more than an education, money, physical beauty, prestigious jobs, or fame.

Common sense constitutes good judgment. Good judgment constitutes good choices. Choices are the key to the quality of our living.

Common sense applies to every area of life at every age of life. We need to learn it, apply it, and teach it to our children. We need to apply common sense to our *thinking*:

> "...not to think more highly of himself than he ought to think, but to think so as to have sound judgment, as God has allotted to each a measure of faith" (Romans 12:3).

> "If anyone thinks he is something when is he nothing, he deceives himself. But let each one examine his own work" (Galatians 6:3,4).

We need to apply common sense to our *mothering*:

> "When I was a child, I used to speak as a child, think as a child, reason as a child; when I became a man, I did away with childish things" (1 Corinthians 13:11).

This verse should speak to us about our expectation levels for our children. Remember, they are children. Also, as mothers we need to give up little-girl thinking and begin thinking in a more mature manner, applying more common sense:

> "Brethren [and women], do not be children in your thinking...*but in your thinking be mature*" (1 Corinthians 14:20).

We need to apply common sense to *reactions*:

"It is good to give *thanks* to the Lord" (Psalm 92:1).

Showing thankfulness and appreciation is a response, a reaction that can be taught. It applies in our relationship to God and in our relationships with other people. When my children receive a gift, I have *taught* them to open it with enthusiasm and to verbally, with eye contact, express appreciation and thanks to the giver. If they act with a "Ho hum, what's in the next package?" attitude, I tactfully remind them to say "thank you" and I make some nice comments about the gift and the giver's thoughtfulness. *After* the party is over I set the child down and recreate the scene—the unappreciative response and the needed proper response. I do not accept excuses like "I *did* like it. I just have a quiet personality."

An appreciative, enthusiastic response is a gift we give back to the giver. God wants us to be thankful for all things, and the only way this can be evident to others is if we show it.

We need to apply *common sense* to our outward expressions and even our facial expressions. As parents we do not allow pouting and sulking. When the girls were small they were spanked for poor attitudes at the dinner table. In the teen years we discipline with different methods, but the rules are the same. Sometimes I have to stand them before a mirror and ask, "Is that a pleasant expression to present to the world?"

Children often have to be taught to be *positive*, to be *enthusiastic*, and to be *smilers*.

We need to apply common sense to our dress. Common sense means understanding the word "appropriate." Children can begin to understand what is appropriate dress for church, appropriate dress for playing in the backyard, and appropriate dress for swimming.

As we discuss the word "appropriate," we can apply it to behavior. There are times to do certain activities and ways to choose particular activities. We teach our children not to accept rides from strangers. We teach them not to throw glass objects. We teach them to keep their pants on in public. This is how they learn common sense.

Common sense, using good judgment, and making good choices are steps up the ladder to *wise living*. Near the top of the ladder, with the help of the Holy Spirit, we catch a glimpse of *wisdom*.

We need to teach our children about Solomon. We pray for wisdom as parents. We must teach our children to pray for wisdom, for wisdom is God-inspired. I believe that wisdom is good judgment combined with God's perfect will. Wisdom is thinking God's thoughts, having God's mind, making God's choices, and expressing God's opinions.

For the first 20 years of my life, my dad discipled me on the basics of common sense and God's wisdom. You would think I'd have it down pat. Instead, I still seek his counsel occasionally, and God's counsel daily. I also seek *insight* from godly friends. I study God's Word for myself. And I review the notes that Dan Jantz dictated to me as he taught me how to make a good decision.

In searching the Scriptures I believe that wisdom begins with how we think and results in how we act. The basics must be the rules of Scripture. There are standards: black and white, right and wrong. First we need to teach our children the absolutes. They must know that God is God. They must know that God is love. They must learn to "love one another, even as I have loved you" (John 13:34).

They must learn that God is just: "It is appointed for men to die once, and after this comes judgment" (Hebrews 9:27).

They must learn the Ten Commandments. As a family, tape them on your refrigerator and memorize them, verse by verse, following dinner each night. Dave and Eunie had their boys memorize a paraphrased version so they could clearly understand the rules.

Once you have taught them the Ten Commandments plus whatever other Scriptures you have selected, continue to review and reinforce and add to these truths until your children know them fully. By teaching Scripture you can continually reinforce that *right is always right.*

Whether at school or in the real world, when your child is making a decision, he will be guided by his knowledge that *right is always right.* This does not guarantee perfect choices and perfect behavior (the prodigal son knew better but chose to go his own way), but it does insure that you as a parent have trained your child in the truths of Scripture. That seed is firmly planted in his heart. Your child may rebel, and you may experience some difficult days, but the last chapter has not been written. Trust God for the last chapter. Trust God for the harvest of your labor. Because of the seeds you plant, your child can always know that *right is always right.*

8

Can't I Pick Your Friends?

How would you like your son to bring home a friend named "Cockroach"? It seems like all of my friends have stories of unusual characters that their kids have brought home. Jason brought home "Moose"—two times the size of Jason! Cindy arrived home with "Miss Queen of the Punkers," a girl with multicolored hair flying in 20 different directions. Clarence eats his lunch every day with "Spike." Our children have brought home friends of every shape and size, color and character, and I begin to panic when their parents don't check up on them after ten hours. It's as bad as bringing home a stray pet!

After meeting a few of these strange friends, I started to think that maybe my younger sister, Adele, had a better thing going when she was a kid. Her "friend," "Johnnie Rotten," didn't have an appealing name, but at least he caused no trouble—he was invisible! He went everywhere with us, and sometimes we had to set a place at the table for Johnnie Rotten. I thought it peculiar at the time, but Adele grew out of it and Johnnie caused a lot less trouble than some of our kids' friends!

Over the years children will invariably pick some friends who would not be our first choice. As mothers we must control our tongues and not run down every selection made. *We will find that very few friends measure up to our own great kids.* Criticizing their choice of friends usually causes more problems than it solves.

Since the days of prearranged marriages, parents have attempted to control the social choices of their children. As a teen, parent-arranged marriages sounded ludicrous to me. Now, as a parent, they don't sound too bad! Seriously, there's too much at stake when we talk about who our child might marry, and even who she might choose as a friend. *Friends influence!*

Friends share not only activities, but also attitudes, likes, dislikes, language, manners, dreams, opinions, and far-out ideas. Because we realize the great influence of friends, we desire to seek the "right kind" of friends for our children. When they are very young, this often means *quiet* children. We avoid "tornadoes" who climb on our furniture, scream and yell, throw toys and books, and cause us to reach for a sedative. This is *not* the influence we want on our child. It's like inviting a headache!

I often wonder if the parents of these kids know how many guest lists they've been scratched off because they have not disciplined their children. The consolation is that *childhood is a process, not a permanent condition.* Children do grow up and can overcome their "bad influence" reputation. I feel badly for the parents who have had to endure those difficult and lonely years when in most cases the problem was correctable.

Choosing Friends

We really can't control who our child chooses for friends at church, at school, or in our neighborhood.

Friendships sometimes form because of similar interests, sometimes because a leader and a follower find each other, and sometimes because the child just happens to sit next to that classmate.

Children don't understand how friendships happen, but they sure don't like us stepping into their private zone and censoring their friends. Yet in this day of drugs, cults, immorality, perversion, and rebellion, we cannot afford to be naive, allowing our kids to be influenced by foolish friends.

As mothers we can encourage deeper friendships with "quality peers" by inviting our choices over whenever appropriate.

"He who walks with wise men will be wise, but the companion of fools will suffer harm" (Proverbs 13:20).

We have found that the easiest way to do this is to invite their families over. By doing an activity or eating a meal together, our children have a natural opportunity to talk, one-on-one, with these chosen guests. Often, after one or two such contacts, a friendship develops that meets with our approval.

Over the years we've found that our children's deepest friendships are with kids they know from both church *and* school. The bonding they experience at church strengthens the support they can give each other at school.

When a situation like this is not possible, we try to center most of our social life around the church. We encourage our children to invite a friend home for dinner on Sunday and let her spend the afternoon. We are not choosing their friends for them but we are providing opportunities for them to choose the *right kind* of close friends.

The Value of Friendships

Many songs about friendships have become popular in recent years. Michael W. Smith's "Friends Forever" was a hit. The secular charts boast "That's What Friends Are For" by Carole Bayer Sager and Burt Bacharach. Even the simple tune "Using Things and Lovin' People, That's the Way It's Got to Be" teaches the value of friendships.

1. *Friends learn to share and get along together.* Beginning with the toddler years, playmates learn the ground rules for sharing toys and getting along with other children. Watching this take place can be more entertaining than going to the movies. The words "no" and "mine" are served into the court and the game is in progress. The players have not read the rules: no pinching...no hitting...no biting...no sitting on another player's head.

As kids get older, they learn to give and take. They learn what's fair and what's not. They learn to overlook unfair treatment at times.

I can recall a day when Tom was a young boy out playing with his neighborhood friends. One playmate had been cruel, mean, unfair, rude, and horrible to Tom. Tom had learned not to fight back in that particular situation. He came running into the house, slammed the door, and announced to his mom, "I can hardly wait for judgment day!"

2. *Friends motivate one another.* As children grow older and learn the rules of the game, they encourage and motivate one another to try activities that they might not try themselves. Eric had fussed and cried when his mom and dad took him swimming. He winced when he got water in his eyes and wouldn't jump off the side of the pool, even when Dad bribed him with a dollar bill.

The following week a number of families enjoyed a barbecue and swim party together. Danny, Eric's buddy, hurled himself into the water and announced that he could swim with his eyes open under water. When Danny did so, the audience of adults applauded. Before long Eric climbed into the water and stuck his face under, eyes open. Before the afternoon was over Eric was jumping off the side of the pool with Danny. The two boys went home that afternoon, eyes blood shot but swimming buddies. Peer motivation was far stronger than the promise of a dollar or the parents' pleading!

3. *Friends educate each other.* As children develop friendships throughout elementary school, they discover on their own the necessary elements of a good friendship. They learn the importance of trust, loyalty, and keeping confidences.

Our children have enjoyed several very special friendships over the years. Cheryl's best friend from when she was in diapers until we moved to Edina when she was 11 was Cindy. Cindy and Cheryl trusted each other and still feel a great sense of loyalty toward each other. Shortly after we moved to Minnesota, Cindy's grandma died very suddenly. Grandma Osterhoudt was like a grandma to our girls during the years we lived in California. Cindy was devastated. Cheryl was devastated. Cindy, within hours of her grandma's death, went into her bedroom, made a cassette tape, and mailed it to Cheryl. On the cassette she tells how terrible she feels, how much she misses her grandma, how she was with her when she died, and how much she wants Cheryl to pray for her grandpa. The tape was one-third talking and two-thirds crying. We cried with Cheryl as we listened to Cindy's sharing and felt the deep friendship that these two girls share.

Cheryl not only has been educated about a valuable friendship; she has experienced different aspects of life through her friend Cindy. This loss and grieving was a part of that education.

I received an education through one of Deanna's friends. Deanna was born with a birthmark, and Lisa was born with cerebral palsy. Before the diagnosis was confirmed, Lisa's mother, Glennyce, visited many doctors. On one occasion Deanna and I traveled to Stanford with Glennyce and Lisa. On another occasion I accompanied them to the Brain Institute in Los Angeles. Our daughters became friends, and Glennyce and I benefited from the emotional support and spiritual strength we could offer each other.

4. *Friends build each other's self-esteem.*

I HAVE A FRIEND

Somebody likes me—I have a friend.
I'm not alone now—he will defend.
He thinks I'm special and worth quite
   a lot.
Maybe I am—he's bright for a tot.

We play together, sharing our toys,
Blending our voices to make lots of noise,
Declaring together what we dream to
   be—
A spaceman, a cowboy, a fireman—maybe.
We know the pressures of being age
   three.
You really don't, cause you're not, you
   see.

My friend understands. He knows what
   it's like

To trip or to fall when riding a trike.
He knows what it's like to stand only so
   tall
And talk to the kneecaps of the rest of
   you all.

He knows what it's like to spend half
   a day
Facing a corner for not wanting to obey,
Thinking what purpose could all of
   this be
When I'd rather, with my friend, be
   climbing a tree.

I have a friend who knows how I feel.
He knows what I like when I'm eating a
   meal.
He knows the fun of just crawling
   around
Pretending we're slithering snakes on
   the ground.

He knows that I know that he likes me a
   lot.
We're buddies, he says, together or not.
He knows that *he's* special, 'cause since
   he likes me,
I quickly decided—his friend to be.

                     —Carol Rischer

A friend your own age understands you better than anyone else does. This is especially true with girls. Two 13-year-olds in the 1980's understand what it feels like to be 13 in the 1980's.

This brings to mind the day Melanie got her first bra. She and her best friend, Kathy, had set the date and made the plans with both moms. Sandy and I arrived at Weinstocks with our two daughters. Melanie and Kathy tried to look calm as they examined bra after bra and finally chose a few to try on. They insisted on going into the dressing rooms alone. Within minutes they changed their minds and were waving for Sandy and me to come and help them decide. I suggested they choose beige bras that wouldn't show under their white blouses. Wouldn't show? After all those years of waiting? Immediately both girls chose white bras.

After the selections were made, we discreetly took them to the checkout counter. The girls tried to look like old pros. The clerk took the money, put the extra bras plus the box from the bra they were each wearing in a bag, then announced, "You girls will find it easier next time." They both died on the spot.

As we walked the mall, Sandy and I couldn't help laughing as we watched these two friends share this day together, especially when Melanie said to Kathy, "Doesn't it make you feel like your belt has slipped up and is strapped around your chest?"

5. *Friends can challenge you.*

"Do you want the truth or a polite answer?"

Only a true friend can tell you the truth, in love, and you can know she's really doing it for your own good.

> "Faithful are the wounds of a friend"
> (Proverbs 27:6).
> "A man's counsel is sweet to his friend"
> (Proverbs 27:9).

Children are often more honest with each other than we are. They are more honest with us than we care for them to be! "Do you want me to tell you what I honestly think?" is enough to cause anyone to break out in a cold sweat. But honesty is what we want. A true friend will be honest in a kind way, because she's already on our side.

The Danger of Friendships

As wonderful and positive as friends can be, they can be equally dangerous if their influence is negative or evil instead of positive and good. It is no secret that drugs have invaded our elementary schools. Many adolescents are sexually active. Lack of respect for authority is a growing influence among young people of today. As these problems get out of control, many parents across the country are throwing up their hands in despair. To give support and strength to these families in crisis, "Tough Love" groups have formed around the country. They provide guidelines to help parents set rules and enforce them.

When parents are asked how their child went astray, the usual response is "peer pressure." This means that their child got into the wrong crowd and had bad friends and bad influences. What's the preventive medicine?

Always know where your children are. Have them ask permission and receive your approval before they go anywhere. If a change of plans should occur, make it a rule that they must notify you. This includes their whereabouts after school. They should be expected to come home unless they call you or you have pre-approved other plans.

Know who your child is with. Always ask who your child has been with. Try to get to know his friends. Invite them into your home so you can determine what type of influence they have on your child.

Talk about quality friends. Don't assume that your child will pick the best friends. Don't assume that your child even knows what to look for in a friend. You might discuss this in a casual way following a television show that depicts friendships. Use teachable moments to point out qualities to be admired or qualities to look out for.

Use the "tough love" approach. If your child and you disagree about a friendship that you believe is potentially dangerous, be firm in your position. Clearly explain your fears and why you are making certain rules about who your child can be with or where your child is allowed to go. Then enforce those rules. You cannot be your child's guardian angel, but you can be a responsible parent.

Family Friendships

While we have let our children enjoy their individual friendships, we have also pursued family friendships. I'm not talking about relatives, although we enjoy a close relationship with both sides of our family. When I talk about family friendships, I mean two families that socialize together.

For years we shared many events with the McEntee family. They had three boys similar in age to our three girls. Since our girls did not have a brother and their boys did not have a sister, we developed this healthy relationship between the families. We were truly blessed by their love, sharing, and wonderful sense of humor. A key to the success of our get-togethers is the amount of laughing we shared as families. The only time we didn't laugh was the time we tried camping together. Sleeping in tents on a Pacific Ocean beach with a cold February breeze blowing and six little explorers kicking sand into our food and coffee is enough to silence any parent's laugh!

When the children were young we joined together

with two other families to form a singing group called The New Covenant Singers. We recorded an album and gave concerts for many years, traveling coast to coast. The Sperlings and Birdsells will forever be precious friends because of the years we spent together as families.

Friends and Finances

The two agencies used to redistribute wealth are taxation and offspring!

My kids are sick of me saying, "We're the Rischers, and we're different."

I got wise to their announcing:

- Everyone has one.
- All the girls are going.
- The whole class gets a ten-dollar allowance.

The "Joneses" may have one, may go somewhere, or may do something, but that has no bearing on what the Rischers will do. As a mother, I have confidently used the word "no" when I believed this answer was in the best interest of the child, the family, and possibly the world. "No" is supposed to be a part of our vocabulary. Contemporary parents seem reluctant to use the authority delegated them. Sometimes areas of conflict are "gray" and need to be discussed and evaluated. Other times we need to stick to our convictions and our budget.

Our two older children now babysit in the neighborhood, clean houses, and do whatever else they can find to earn money. Boys can cut grass, shovel snow, or ride a paper route. Sometimes kids can make more money than they can handle. The Kelbys gave us an idea that we have applied to our household, and so far it's worked beautifully.

We impose a 50 percent "set-aside" tax on all monies our kids earn. This set-aside money prepares them for the real world, teaches them some valuable lessons about budgeting, and still allows them to buy some things they want.

Economists advise: If you plan to teach your children the value of a dollar, you better do it quick!

Friends and Hospitality

As much as I love formal dinner settings with fine china, crystal, silverware, and soft music, much of my entertaining is casual. One or two nights a week one of the children has a friend over for dinner or we invite a family over to share food and fellowship. Families with children understand casual dinners with interrupted conversations and regular cleanups during the meal. Still, this is a good time to instruct our children on proper etiquette, polite table conversation, and how to build friendships.

At formal dinner parties I allow our children to "entertain" the guests while I put the final touches on the meal. Usually they'll sing or play the piano, violin, or flute. Sometimes they talk; this causes me to hurry in the kitchen! Bill Butterworth suggests posting a sign:

> THE VIEWS EXPRESSED BY THE
> CHILDREN OF THIS HOUSEHOLD
> DO NOT NECESSARILY REFLECT
> THOSE OF THE MANAGEMENT.

However we entertain, whether formal or casual, we model hospitality for our children.

> "... contributing to the needs of the saints, practicing hospitality" (Romans 12:13).

"Do not neglect to show hospitality to strangers, for by this some have entertained angels without knowing it" (Hebrews 13:2).

My husband says we haven't met any angels yet, but we've entertained some strange kids! I reminded him of this verse:

"Be hospitable to one another without complaint" (1 Peter 4:9).

Overnight Guests

When we have company, we all get involved in washing sheets, cleaning rooms, putting extra hangers in the guest room closet, laying fresh towels on the guest's bed, putting fresh flowers in a vase in the room, making a welcome sign, and planning the menu. One reason we've had so many overnight guests is because we moved 2500 miles from family and friends in Canada. Their visits are one way we've stayed close. Occasionally I've wondered when a child's enthusiasm for giving up her bedroom and doubling up in sister's room would become a negative. We recently had two weeks of overnight guests, and the girls all begged for the honor of letting the guests stay in *their* room.

Having overnight visitors gets easier as the kids grow older. When children are very young they can react negatively because they don't get to bed on time, and the confusion of extra noise and activity in the house makes them upset and cranky. Guests think they see us at our best, but they really don't. Our house is a little more cluttered because of the luggage and extra people. Our children are overtired and more irritable because of the disruption of their schedule. We can be a little on edge with our husbands because we're worried about the children's behavior and the quality and variety of the meals and how we look, and on and on.

The only advice I can give is: *Relax.* Prepare ahead as much as possible, then roll with the punches. Try to enjoy the time. Your guests should be there to enjoy you and your children—not to inspect the house, assess your cooking, check out your schedule, evaluate how you discipline your children, and grade your overall entertaining skills. If they do that, they're not true friends, even if they're family.

Family Vacations

As difficult as they are to save for, we make family vacations a priority each year. This is the time to escape from our regular environment and enjoy a different and refreshing time together.

I've already related how during the 20 years at home with my parents, vacations were a highlight. We were fortunate to have a summer house, and we still enjoy family reunions there every summer. Not everyone has that luxury, but there are inexpensive alternatives that allow for quality family time. Many families go to church family camp together. Others rent a cabin and spend a week or two away from it all. Still others go camping with a tent or camper.

Vacations will make for some of your children's greatest memories. When I was a child, in addition to the summer home, our family (seven of us in a car) traveled to Texas and Florida one year, California another, British Columbia another. I remember Disneyland, the Grand Canyon, and the Gulf of Mexico. More than that, I remember singing and harmonizing in the car, telling stories, telling jokes, talking about the Lord, discussing prophecy, and playing games. Sometimes we fought and spilled our milkshakes in the car and argued about whose turn it was to sit by the window or ride in the front seat. But we also built solid relationships and now share memories that will last a lifetime. There's nothing like being locked up together with no telephone and no TV!

You don't need to make a vacation a two-or-three-week ordeal. If budget is a problem, think small. Living in California provided us many opportunities to take minivacations—weekends in Carmel, days at Disneyland, trips to the mountains. It's worth the sacrifice and saving and planning.

Friends and the Good Life

Christian families should not only pray together but enjoy life together. Christian friends are usually our closest friends because we can share what's closest to our hearts. But we need to be careful that we have balance. At one time as a child I attended a church that was very conservative and very serious. These godly men and women focused on keeping themselves holy and pure. They kept an unwritten list of "don'ts" that made them feel God was happier with them than with other people. The problem was that I was more interested in *doing* than *don'ting*. My sisters and I used to rehearse a poem:

My mother taught me not to smoke.
I don't.
Or listen to a dirty joke.
I don't.
She made it clear
I must not think about intoxicating drink.
I don't. . . .

The poem goes on to list all the "don'ts" and finally ends with:

> You wouldn't think I have much fun.
> I don't.

That typified so many Christians I knew. It's not that my sisters and I wanted to do anything *bad*—we just wanted to focus on things we *did* rather than things we *didn't*. I've never tried a cigarette or tasted beer. That doesn't make me a goody-goody. Whether I did or didn't is not the issue. The point is that I don't want my life to be represented by what I *do*—living the *abundant life*. I want to involve my children in the abundant life so they will continue to celebrate life with me and share this good news with other people.

Many Christians say they have something wonderful to share with the world, but they don't get close enough to share it because they might come in contact with a "don't." This wasn't Jesus' example. I'm glad my parents were *doers* and reared us to be *doers*. To this day, all five of us girls are living for the Lord and doing His will.

Many second-generation Christians with whom I grew up are not living for the Lord today. Some who claim to are living superficial lives. They show up at their parents' church on Sundays, but carouse the rest of the week, indulging in all the "don'ts" they were forbidden to do as young people.

Each family must choose their own standards for recreation and socialization. But let's focus on *doing*, on celebrating the best life that is available only to true born-again believers who love living for their Lord. Let's save our "don'ts" for obeying God's rules, keeping the Ten Commandments, and the black-and-whites of Scripture. It's confusing for a child to grow up believing that bowling is sinful only to find out it's not, to grow up believing that pool tables are of the devil, that swimming on Sunday is a rule that God forgot to tell us, and that movies are all bad so don't step into a theater. Movies are not all bad—only 95 percent of them are. Immorality and murder and taking God's name in vain are sin, and most movies contain these, so we avoid this negative environment. When something is to be avoided, let's explain *why* to our children. As they grow older they will use these same reasons to determine what is right and wrong for them.

For every negative we cannot do, there are so many positives we *can* do. Enjoying the good life is part of God's plan for us. Let's transmit love of the good to our kids.

9

Thus Saith the Lord

Spiritual Development

"Does your family have family devotions?" asked Sammy.

"We sure do!" replied George. "We watch the Waltons together every week."

The spiritual development of our children has a different meaning to each family. Often what we intend to teach is not what the children learn. That can make for some humorous situations. Heidi was so excited when she came home from Sunday school because she had memorized a verse. Patti, her mother, asked her to quote it. Heidi hesitated, trying to get it straight in her mind, then proudly said, "Don't worry, guys—you'll get the blanket."

Confused and concerned, Patti called the teacher to find out what was actually taught. It all became clear when the teacher quoted the actual verse: "Fear not, brethren, for the comforter shall come."

Sometimes we realize what the kids are learning by the pictures they draw. Ryan drew a picture of an airplane with a man driving, and presented it to his mom. "Who's this?" she asked. Ryan thought it was obvious: "It's Pontius the Pilot!"

When Glenna was very young, she drew a picture of a car with a man driving and a man and woman sitting in the backseat. Her dad, Glen, had preached in church that Sunday and asked her to take notes. "What is this?" he politely asked. She replied, "It's God driving Adam and Eve out of the garden of Eden."

Have you ever wondered what Jesus' growing-up years might have been like? It's hard for us to think of Christ as an active little boy or as a teenager. We can't imagine rearing a perfect child.

Luke 2:39-52 shares a few insights into Jesus' youth, but very few. Verse 39 reveals that Mary and Joseph performed everything according to the "law of the Lord" during those early years. But they were not perfect parents; only Jesus was perfect. Chuck Swindoll in *You and Your Child* points out that perfect Jesus, the Son of God, was reared in the home of imperfect parents, and He willingly subjected Himself to their authority.

We, as equally imperfect parents, can seek to rear our children by "the law of the Lord," teaching them what their heavenly Father desires. Let's examine some ways to do that.

Spiritual Teaching

"Hear, my son, your father's instruction, and *do not forsake your mother's teaching*" (Proverbs 1:8).

We as mothers are to teach our children. This can happen during a time of *formal* instruction each day, or through a short devotional following a family meal, or once a week during family worship and study time.

We are also instructed to *informally* teach our children:

"You shall teach them diligently to your sons [and daughters] and shall talk of them when you sit in your house and when you walk by the way and when you lie down and when you rise up" (Deuteronomy 6:7).

This happens as we talk about the Lord openly and naturally around our house. It also happens by using "teachable moments" to teach about the Lord. When telling about the day's events, we might express "God did such a neat thing for me today." When helping a student with a homework assignment we can suggest, "Let's ask God to help us understand this and do a good job." When consoling a crying child we can affirm, "God loves you and I love you. What can we do to help you?" This kind of daily conversation teaches us at least as much as our times of formal instruction.

Family Devotions

Family devotions have the power to bind a family together or to bore a family to tears! What's appropriate depends on the age of our children, their attention span, their needs, our needs, and our schedules. Some families spend one evening a week in Bible study and worship (chorus singing, praying, praising), followed by snacks or a fun outing. Other families take a few minutes each night after dinner or before bed. Because our evenings are often taken with church meetings or Paul's counseling or hospital visitation, we try to have our family devotions following breakfast.

Paul has used different materials for family devotions, but one of our favorites is *The Family Walk*, put out by the publishers of *The Daily Walk*. This devotional takes about ten minutes. It's contemporary and relevant, and contains Scripture reading and questions for discussion. We end with prayer for the day.

We have another prayer time after dinner when we pray for missionaries, pastors, family, and friends. Over the years we've refined our system. We collect pictures of all the people we want to pray for and laminate them on a 3 x 5 card. We put them in a nice basket and after dinner pass the basket around the table. Each family member selects a card and prays for that person.

If we have company for dinner, I often choose a theme and look up verses that deal with that topic. I've used topics such as "Rejoice," "Thankfulness," "Love" (decorating the table with hearts), "Angels" (using an angel as a centerpiece), or "Sheep" (using sheep-shaped name tags). Once I choose my theme, I take my Bible and, using the concordance, copy some verses that teach on that subject. I write each verse on a 3 x 5 recipe card and hide one or two under each dinner plate. Occasionally I choose one large passage and copy one verse to each card.

Between dinner and dessert, Paul has us look under our plates. We go around the table reading the Scripture verses related to our theme for the meal. I save my 3 x 5's, so over the years I've collected an assortment of theme verses. This method of family Bible reading allows everyone to participate without intimidating or embarrassing guests, especially if they're not believers. When people read their verse, they are welcome to make a comment about the passage if they want to. Paul usually closes this time of devotion with a prayer of thanksgiving or dedication.

Scripture Memorization

For 11 summers as a child I attended Faith Bible

Camp. A scholarship was offered to those who memorized 100 verses and quoted them accurately, word for word. Even though I knew my parents were going to donate my camp fee, they required me to complete the Scripture memorization each year. To this day those verses remain clear in my mind and heart. One woman I know set chapters of Scripture to familiar tunes when her children were growing up. That's a great way to memorize.

We have tried rewards to motivate us. One summer the McEntee family challenged our family to memorize a particular psalm. That fall each family member quoted what they learned to the other family. The family that memorized the least treated the family that memorized the most to a McDonald's supper.

Another spiritual project that our family has developed involves specific character traits. We choose one characteristic, such as patience, self-control, or kindness, and post it on the refrigerator door for a week. We learn a Scripture verse along with that trait. For example:

> "This you know, my beloved brethren. But let everyone be *quick to hear, slow to speak,* and *slow to anger*" (James 1:19).

As you can see, these projects are not just aimed at helping our kids!

Family Council

Once a week our family sits around the kitchen table to review rules, debate issues, and vent any complaints. It's an opportunity for any family member to get something off her chest. We keep a "Family Council" three-ringed notebook where we write down any rules we decide upon or document any decisions that are made.

This avoids arguments such as "I didn't think you said *that*" or "I thought I was only grounded three days, not the whole week!"

In our notebook we have written our family goal:

> "If therefore there is any encouragement in Christ, if there is any consolation of love, if there is any fellowship of the Spirit, if any affection and compassion, make my joy complete by being of the same mind, maintaining the same love, united in spirit, intent on one purpose. Do nothing from selfishness or empty conceit, but with humility of mind let each of you regard one another as more important than himself; do not merely look out for your own personal interests, but also for the interests of others" (Philippians 2:1-4).

Here is another goal that we chose:

> "Bearing with one another, and forgiving each other; whoever has a complaint against anyone; just as the Lord forgave you, so also should you" (Colossians 3:13).

This council lasts an hour at the most. Some weeks it's not necessary to meet. But any family member can call a council at any time. Because of our schedules we usually meet Saturdays at 11 A.M., right after brunch. Other families have it during "family night" or after devotions.

Family Night

"It's your week, Cheryl. Have you decided where we're going?" I asked.

"Bowling."

"What a riot. I haven't bowled in years!"

"Then we're coming back here to make popcorn balls."

"Sounds like a good choice!"

Deanna piped in, "It's my turn next week, and we're going to the zoo!"

Periodically one family member gets to choose a family activity for "family night." One week Melanie chose roller-skating, and I think Paul and I enjoyed it more than the kids! Paul chose a barbecue in the park and Cheryl got bit by a goose. The family booed and hissed when I announced that for my turn we were all going to clean the garage. It turned out better than it sounded. That Saturday we played music, laughed and talked, discovered all sorts of lost treasures, and ordered pizza for lunch.

We do not do this year-round. Some weeks take care of themselves—there's a carnival at school, or a family outing at church, or we all want to go ice skating, or we all decide to bike ride over to one of the lakes. Our goal is to spend some time enjoying life together each week. We try to spend one night each week, or Saturday, with everyone in the family together for an activity. Besides giving us fun times, the more our children see us in all areas of living, the more receptive they'll be to our spiritual teaching.

Nonverbal Teaching

"If you can't say something nice then don't say anything at all," children hear us preach. Then they hear us gossip about neighbors or business associates, tearing them to shreds.

"Never, never lie. Always tell the truth," we preach. Then we tell them to say they're two years younger so we can order from the child's menu at the restaurant, or save money on the purchase of an airline ticket.

"Read your Bible every day," sounds so right when we say it. Why don't they see us doing it?

"Respect authority and obey your teachers" loses its punch when Dad tells off those in authority over him.

"Church is very important, so be good in Sunday school today" holds less weight when Dad and Mom drop off the kids at church for free babysitting and go out for coffee.

ACTIONS SPEAK LOUDER THAN WORDS.
"BY THEIR ACTS YE SHALL KNOW THEM."

As adults, we're quick to recognize hypocrisy in another person. Some adults use "hypocrites" as their excuse for not going to church or not progressing in their spiritual lives. As quickly as we recognize a hypocrite and negate what he represents, so does a child. The easiest way to lead our child to Christ is to live for Christ before his eyes.

Choosing a Church

Our child needs the support of a good, solid, Bible-believing, on-fire-for-the-Lord, caring church. And so do we. The church is not a building; the church is God's people. We gather together in little clusters across our cities and country. Choose a church whose doctrinal statement coincides with your convictions, whose style of worship enhances your own, whose preacher is a Bible scholar and mature in his teaching, and whose people show Christ's love. You need this kind of church, and so do your children.

Beyond our church, we need to expose our family to Christian missionaries, Christian organizations, Christian music concerts, and Christian books. *Expand your child's vision of what God is doing in this world.*

When I was a teenager and first attended a Youth

for Christ rally, I met people from many different denominations who claimed to be Christians. At first I thought they couldn't be Christians as "our church" meant it. They couldn't be born again. They couldn't be as close to God as my church was. But they were! Many were more mature in their Christian walk and had a greater vision of what God could do through them in our city. And He was doing it!

Leading Your Child to Christ

As a mother, I can think of no greater fulfillment than the privilege of leading my children to the Lord. I can distinctly remember the day that each of our daughters prayed to receive Christ.

Melanie was nearly four years old. This is *very* young for a child, but she had heard the story of Jesus since she was born. One Sunday she came home from Sunday school, ate dinner, and was put on her bed for our traditional Sunday afternoon nap. A half-hour later she came into our room where I was resting and said she couldn't sleep because she wanted to ask Jesus into her heart. Her Sunday school teacher had talked about it that morning and she couldn't get it out of her mind. We reviewed what it meant to become a Christian, why Jesus had died and why He rose again, and how He personally cared about her. Then we knelt by the bed and she prayed and received Christ. Later that day we wrote out what she had done. She wrote down (as I called out the letters) that she had asked Jesus into her heart, and the date—March 18, 1976—then signed her name. We keep this record in a plastic cover in her baby book.

Cheryl's decision came on December 21, 1976, as we were driving down First Street in Fresno. Melanie was talking about being a Christian when Cheryl asked if everyone in the family was a Christian. I explained that each person must individually ask Jesus into her heart. We pulled off First Street and stopped the car. I told Cheryl I would pray for her first and then she could pray. She replied, "Don't pray for me, Mom. Pray for yourself!" Then she proceeded to pray and asked Jesus into her life. When we got home, we recorded her decision with the date and her signature in her baby book.

Deanna made her commitment to Christ on August 21, 1981. She had gone with me to the hairdresser and watched as I had my hair cut and witnessed to my beautician. On the way home Deanna asked question after question, then announced that she was going to pray right there and ask Jesus into her heart. Again I found myself pulling off the road and praying with Deanna as she joined God's forever family. We drove home and recorded her decision so she might feel secure in her early commitment.

While my girls came to Christ early in life, every child is different. Let me share ways that your child might accept Christ.

God uses you and others to teach your child about Himself and Jesus Christ dying for your child's soul. God also speaks to your child through the Holy Spirit, causing him to recognize a need in his life. In order to make a decision, a child needs to have a basic understanding of what "becoming a Christian" means. Some experts feel that a child reaches full understanding at around age seven. Some feel a child reaches accountability at age 12. God alone knows when each child comes to full awareness of his need for God and a decision to neglect or accept what Christ provides.

If your child believes when he is very young, accept his innocent faith and allow it to grow and blossom. Do not negate a decision he wants to make because you feel he's too young. If your child is older and has not made a decision for Christ, *do not force the issue*. Pray and wait patiently for the Holy Spirit to work in your child's life.

It's a wonderful blessing when you can lead your child to Christ. But if your child is led to the Lord by a Sunday school teacher or a friend or an evangelist, praise the Lord! This was God's timing, and your child responded. Remember, the Holy Spirit alone causes a person to respond to God. People—including parents— are used to teach and encourage, but God alone gets credit for the results. This continues through the spiritual growth of your child:

> "Neither the one who plants nor the one who waters is anything, but God who causes the growth" (1 Corinthians 3:7).

This verse should be a comfort to us. We can teach, encourage, model, and pray. But let's leave the results up to God.

When Did You Pray to Receive Christ?

I was very fortunate to be reared in a Christian home. While I was growing up, my parents constantly talked to me about the Lord and prayed with me each night as I went to bed. Day after day, year after year, I prayed, "Please forgive me of my sins. Come into my heart, Lord Jesus." I sincerely meant these prayers. I do not know of the actual day I accepted Christ, and it doesn't really matter. I *do* know that I asked Jesus to live in my heart, and I know He does so now. As I grew in my understanding of God, I recommitted my life to Him at camp and at Youth for Christ rallies, surrendering areas that I recognized needed to be under His lordship. My Christian faith grew as I grew in my understanding. I did not have a date for the people who would corner me with the question "When were you saved?" But I had confidence in my personal commitment to God.

Many children today do not feel as secure in their commitments. Anything we can do to strengthen their faith is a worthwhile investment. *If* you are aware of the day your child prays to receive Christ, document this and have your child sign his name. Then begin to celebrate his decision.

Celebrating Christianity

Since I know the dates my children prayed to receive Christ, our family celebrates spiritual birthdays! This isn't something out of the Bible, but then neither are Sunday evening services, midweek services, or organized youth programs. This is simply one way our family celebrates our Christianity.

We do not involve friends or outsiders—we reserve "friends and presents" parties for their physical birthdays. We *do* have a family party, complete with streamers and balloons and one special gift from Dad and Mom. It's a fun day, focusing on one child and the Lord's presence in that child's life. The benefits of celebrating spiritual birthdays are many:

1. This celebration creates an openness regarding their faith as we remember the decision made and prayers prayed.

2. This often creates an openness with our children's friends. At school they've explained, "We're having a party at our house. This is the birthday of the day I asked Jesus into my heart," or, "I have a new dress. It's my gift for my spiritual birthday." This openness often develops into interesting discussions

with classmates. One teacher overheard Melanie's conversation and said in front of the class, "Your spiritual birthday? Ha! What are you talking about?" Melanie responded to a hushed class, "I'm a Christian, and my spiritual birthday marks the day that I asked Jesus into my heart." The discussion continued, and Melanie was able to share her faith in a secular public school setting!

3. Our celebration adds to each child's security in remembering the important decision she made. When she has doubts, as all children do, she can reread her insert in her baby book. We can discuss it. However, if a child is plagued by doubt and wants to "pray again," let her, and then record this new commitment.

4. Having a spiritual decision recorded often helps in witnessing or giving a testimony. When Melanie has been asked to share her testimony at church or Sunday school, she takes along her scribbled memo written the day she first prayed to receive Christ.

5. Celebrating spiritual birthdays reinforces the fact that our Christianity is something worth celebrating. This is the greatest thing in life! It's more exciting than a football game. More fun than a party. More important than money. More necessary than education. More precious than the most intimate family relationships. More valuable than any other possession on this earth.

Celebrating our faith isn't limited to our spiritual birthdays. There are many other opportunities. We use a "YOU ARE SPECIAL TODAY" red plate for special occasions. This plate comes out for birthdays, special guests, and definitely on spiritual birthdays. During dinner we go around the table and give each family member a chance to say why they think that person is special. This is a good exercise on focusing on the positives. No child is perfect, but each is *special*.

Sandy made us a tiny, heart-shaped pillow with a

cross-stitched message: "I did it because I love you." Sometimes the gifts we give our children are not materialistic—they're intangible acts of love. Our pillow floats around the house, landing on a bed made as a surprise for another, sitting by a plate of freshly baked cookies, lying by a dress freshly pressed for a daughter who's behind schedule, sitting on a counter by the sink where the pots and pans no longer sit soaking. It's a fun way to express our love for God and for each other every day. And isn't that what it really means to celebrate Christianity?

Teach Me to Pray

Randy and Darlene were making a major decision regarding Randy's business. As they were on their knees praying, their three-year-old daughter Tara came into the room and knelt down beside them. Randy and Darlene continued to pray, asking God to open doors for them if they were to expand in a certain direction. When it came Tara's time to pray, she asked God to please open all the doors and windows for Daddy.

On one occasion when we were guests at a friend's home, one of our daughters was asked to pray. She proceeded, "Dear Father, thank You for the nice day, and for our friends and for this nice supper: the meat and the juice and the (I couldn't help but notice her eyes peeking)...uh...jelly salad and the...oh, no... yech!...not the carrots! AMEN." Now that was truly a prayer from the heart!

If the disciples needed instruction in praying, our children certainly could benefit from the teaching. We might even learn something ourselves!

1. *Begin praying for your child daily—from the moment you know you are pregnant until the last day*

of your life. The knowledge that you pray daily will motivate your child to pray daily. Actions speak louder than words. Words produce action when said in a prayer.

2. *Pray with your child before each meal.* This is the easiest time to teach your child to pray. We have never used memorized prayers, but have always encouraged our children to pray what they are thinking. Praying is just talking to God. These prayers are more meaningful to the child—and more interesting to the adults.

Sometimes, rather than pray before a meal, we sing a song. The chorus "God Is So Good" acknowledges our thankfulness to God.

Usually we hold hands around the table as we pray. Sometimes that's the only time all day that we're together. If guests are present, we include them in our holding of hands and prayer time.

We usually take turns leading in prayer. When I was a child growing up there were seven in the family, so we each had a day of the week when we asked the blessing.

3. *Pray with your child before bedtime.* Sometimes with our busy schedules this is difficult to do consistently. As much as is possible, tuck your child into bed each evening with a hug, a kiss, and a prayer.

Kneeling with our child by his bed can provide an important memory as he recalls our humbling ourselves and acknowledging our need of God in both of our lives.

When you can't be with your child at bedtime, teach him to pray before he falls asleep. If you're with him 90 percent of the evenings, he should learn the habit.

4. *Pray with your child whenever the need arises.* Presently my children's school has a prayer chain consisting of Christian teachers and mothers. As needs arise at school the teachers record them, and once a

week they are called through the prayer chain. Some of these mothers also meet one morning a week for corporate prayer for the schoolchildren.

When a prayer-chain request is called in to me that I feel free to share with my children, I ask whoever is home and available to take a couple of minutes, kneel with me by the couch, and join me in prayer. Because of these experiences, my children often come to me with a problem and say, "Can we pray about _____?" The answer is always "yes."

5. *Pray with your child in group situations.* There is a difference between healthy fear and being scared to death of a situation. Whether we're talking about swimming, riding a horse, performing on a stage in front of people, or *praying in public*, a child needs to learn to cope. In many instances, these fears can be overcome when the children are very young, saving them years of embarrassing agony.

This applies to getting over the fright of praying in front of other people. If you pray before meals, always give your child a turn. When company comes, continue to give him his turn. If he resists, don't force it or embarrass him. Continue to give him a chance and slowly build his confidence. We've also been in multi-family situations where we've let each person in each family pray a short prayer out loud. Used sensitively, this is a wonderful growing experience for all.

When we give a concert as a family, we always gather together first and have each person pray. Here there are no exceptions; we dare not sing or share without God's help. When we sang with two other families as part of The New Covenant Singers, each performance was preceded by prayer. "Young" prayers were as meaningful as "old" prayers...often more meaningful.

I would encourage you to provide opportunities for

your children to learn to pray: individually and corporately, in private and in public. In every situation, *teaching your child to pray is teaching your child to rely on God.*

What About Santa Claus and the Easter Bunny?

How do we teach our child what is real and what is not? Do we confuse our children with all the frivolous festivities included in our year? Or do we make our children resent their Christianity because we require them to "abstain" from these evil childhood fantasies? Do we make another list of "don'ts" and add a few more "no's"?

I have seen both extremes abused. If we are total abstainers in a gray area where 90 percent of the children in our society participate, we risk becoming "holier than thou" and turning off the younger generation. Some families in the extremely conservative church where I grew up forbid their children from participating in any "worldly celebrations." Santa Claus never came to their house. The Easter Bunny was not mentioned. The idea of a Fairy Godmother was openly scoffed. These were the same children who were not allowed to go to a show, to dance, to play pool, or to swim on Sunday.

Twenty years later a generation of rebellious teens have broken out of their legalistic cages and secretly participated in sins far worse than their parents imagined. They still show up at church occasionally, which pleases their parents, but that is the depth of their Christianity.

It's equally dangerous to pretend that the Easter Bunny or Santa Claus is real. To say that Santa Claus "is watching you" in order to make a child behave during the Christmas season can confuse his image of

God. I prefer to let childhood fun be childhood fun—not to be confused with *real life* and our *real God.*

How can we do this? We read fairy tales and nursery rhymes to our little ones. We play "imaginary" games. It's fun to use our imagination, but we know it's only pretend. We can keep the balance by explaining the truth learned in a story, or by relating a similar character in history. Stories about why we do certain fun things—like decorating the Christmas tree, putting out our stockings, and receiving surprise gifts—can add to a child's appreciation of the traditions of Christmas.

The most important thing is: *Never confuse the real meaning of a holiday with the fun activities we do.* When we talk about Christmas, we should talk ten times more about the birth of Baby Jesus than about the fun of finding our stockings filled by Santa Claus. The following are a few ideas to help us convey the true meaning of Christmas and Easter to our children.

1. *Planning Christmas.*

• Decorate around the theme of Jesus' birth and the angels rejoicing. (But I wouldn't forbid a Santa in the house.)

• Plan special family devotions for the month of December. You could use *Family Walk* or an advent calendar and advent candles, and have a special reading each evening.

• Make a birthday card for Jesus, telling Him how much you love Him.

• Read the Christmas story as part of your Christmas celebration. A number of years ago I printed Luke 2:1-20 on twenty 3 x 5 cards. On Christmas Day I place these cards in order under each dinner plate. After our first course, we go around the table and read the Christmas story together.

• Bake a birthday cake for Jesus and sing Happy Birthday to Him at your Christmas dinner table. We have done this for years. I love watching the expressions on my daughters' faces when I ask them to write "HAPPY BIRTHDAY, JESUS," in icing on the cake.

• Gift wrap an empty box, complete with bow and tag. On the tag write "TO JESUS FROM THE _____ FAMILY." Cut a slit in the top of the box and ask each member of the family to write down and insert what he or she would like to give Jesus. They can write one or more gifts and add them at any time until Christmas day.

During the Christmas celebration, open this special gift together and read what each person gave Jesus. Those marked "personal" should not be read aloud. Here are some of the kinds of gifts we give to Jesus:

• Visit a senior citizens' home.
• Give one of my good toys to a poor family.
• Help a neighbor clean her house or babysit her children.
• Help a neighbor shovel his driveway or weed his garden.
• Wash the kitchen floor for Mommy.
• Write a letter to a missionary.

Before the New Year, we help our children schedule these activities:

• Give a prayer of praise and thanksgiving to God for Jesus Christ.
• Sing Christmas carols together.
• Share Christmas with other people.

The highlight of our Christmas celebration is caroling as a family. We set aside one, two, sometimes three evenings before Christmas to visit nearby neighborhoods and sing. We *don't* go to our friends' houses—they know we love them. We go to senior citizens' homes, convalescent hospitals, and homes of the terminally ill.

We always sing traditional Christmas carols, and the past several years we've ended with a song I wrote for these outreach occasions:

HAPPY BIRTHDAY TO JESUS

Jesus' birthday is here;
It's the time of the year when we say "Merry
   Christmas" and wish all good cheer.
We clean and we bake and we all decorate.
But what can we do to help God celebrate?

Chorus

We'll sing "Happy Birthday" to Jesus.
We'll have a long talk with Him too.
As a gift to Him I'll wrap up myself—
And live for Him all my life through.
As husband and wife we'll thank Jesus
For giving us peace so true.
If you will accept God's gift of love,
Then Christmas will bring peace to you.

We'll have turkey and dressing and cranberry
   jelly,
Candy canes, cookies, and Santa's fat belly—
Memories so precious they still linger on.
But what really counts after Christmas is
   gone?

Take time this Christmas to thank God the
   Father
For sending His Son to earth,
For letting Him live and for letting Him die
That we might experience new life through
   rebirth.

— Carol Rischer

When children awaken early on Christmas morning to see what Santa has put in their stockings, they have fun and don't feel left out of the good things in a kid's life. But they're also learning the better and best things. They don't focus on the fun of Santa, but on the fact that this is a celebration of the birthday of Jesus Christ.

2. *Planning Easter.* For us as Christians, Easter should be a far greater celebration than Christmas. One way to do this is to dye your eggs and hold your Easter egg hunt on Saturday. Reserve Sunday for your special worship service—whether a sunrise service in the park or a grand church service at your church. Some families also celebrate communion together in their homes. Whatever ways we choose to teach and celebrate Easter with our children, let's keep this day focused on our resurrected Lord.

A most meaningful part of Easter for our family is attending Easter pageants, cantatas, and musicals. The dramatic presentations depicting Jesus' last days before the cross, His death on the cross, and His resurrection bring to life the reality of what took place 2000 years ago. Whether small church productions or glorious extravaganzas, the visual message will remain in your child's mind and heart.

The children's director at our church, prepares an Easter Family Devotional Guide for our church families to use the week before Easter. She gives suggested Bible readings such as Mark 11:1-11 and Mark 14:32-42 plus questions for discussion. She suggests making a family mural and adding to the story each day after the devotion time.

Other ideas you might try include acting out some of the events of Holy Week, drawing pictures of the Last Supper, discussing why the Passover meal is called the Last Supper, making a family prayer list after studying Jesus' prayer in the Garden of Gethsemane, drawing a picture of Jesus dying on the cross, and finally having a family service on Easter Sunday in which you praise God that Jesus rose from the dead and is alive today and living in heaven.

Begin on Palm Sunday to focus on Jesus' last week on earth: His last supper and His death, burial, and resurrection. Build your own traditions in making this the greatest celebration of your year.

Conversational Teaching

Much of what your child learns about God he will learn from conversations. That's why it's so important to let God be a part of your everyday, natural conversation. Some of the songs I've written have come out of conversations with my daughters.

We were out fishing late one July night on Lake of the Woods. Cheryl was sitting on my knee, quite concerned that it was now very dark. This led into a conversation about her being afraid of the dark. Later that night I wrote this song based on our discussion:

> When God turns out the lights at night and I
>   lay down to sleep,
> I close my eyes but they won't stay, and I
>   don't like counting sheep.
> So I think about my family and the world
>   that I live in,
> And I think about tomorrow and how today
>   has been.
>
> Chorus:
>
> And God, I feel You near me.
> You said You'd never leave me by myself.
> I thank You for the fun times You give me.

I know it's You who gives me my health.

I think about how great and handsome You
  must be,
And I'm really glad to know You care so
  much for me.
I get out of my bed to talk to You on
  my knees.
For I really do love You so.

Children have such uninhibited faith! We sometimes
chuckle and think "How impossible!" Yet the Scriptures teach that all we need is to have the faith of a
little child. Our middle daughter has a burden for her
unsaved friends. When our junior high youth group
planned an all-night evangelistic outreach party,
Cheryl and her friend, Sarah, invited 50 classmates.
They even had faith that they would show up. Paul
and I were a little skeptical and hoped the girls
wouldn't be disappointed. The girls prayed and
believed. The evening of the "blitz" 42 of their
classmates came, and many prayed to receive Christ!
After that a Bible study for new believers was started.
Cheryl and Sarah's faith challenged us parents.

The more we converse, the more I can teach my
children and the more they can share their thoughts
with me. I can't help them with their fears and doubts
and confusion if they don't make me aware of these
thoughts.

Learning from Our Children

We are required as mothers to teach our children.
What a surprise it is to discover that we also learn from
our children! They are so sincere, so honest, so full of
hope and faith. Jesus recognized this:

"He called a child to Himself and set him
before them, and said, 'Truly I say to you,
unless you are converted and become like
children, you shall not enter the kingdom of
heaven' " (Matthew 18:2).

I have two goals in life—what I call my "M & M's."
Some of you are probably guessing "Motherhood and
Marriage." That's not it, but my two goals *will* enhance
the effectiveness and success in my marriage and
mothering.

In listing the many and varied activities that make
up my day-to-day life as a mother, you might have
guessed that one of my life goals is collecting *MEMO-
RIES*. What is each day beyond a memory? "Memories"
is my *second* goal in life—providing meaningful
memories for my family and friends.

Goal number one? It's to reach *MATURITY*. Don't
laugh. Some adults never reach it. They live their
entire life dependent on other people, never accepting full responsibility for their own lives. I'm not
suggesting that we can live without other people. I am
saying that these adults continue to blame other people,
circumstances, hardships, their background, or their
environment for the way they are. They constantly
tell you *why* it's someone else's fault that they couldn't
succeed or be a more caring person:

- My parents never took me to church, so
  you can't expect me to begin now.
- I grew up in the ghetto, so you can't expect
  me to be successful.
- My father always demanded that my
  mother wait on him, so I'm never going to
  let my husband tell me what to do.

- I was a terror when I was a little girl, so I'm not surprised that my little girl is a brat too.
- My husband is immoral, so I might as well be too.
- Our family has always been prejudiced against (whatever minority or nationality).

I'm sure your list of excuses for immature thinking isn't as blatant as the above. But if you and I are honest, there are still areas where we avoid accepting responsibility, especially when we consider our spiritual lives. We cannot rely on someone else's beliefs to get us into heaven. As a mother I can't say to God, "I didn't accept You as my God because I was so busy having kids and my husband was so demanding. Between the pressures from him, my children, and my bridge club (I needed *some* relaxation), plus my part-time job, there was no time to get to know You."

I'd like to challenge you to do a little exercise that has greatly benefited me. Sit down for a few minutes and think of areas where you accept full responsibility and feel mature. Then write down areas where you have avoided responsibility and now feel embarrassed about your immaturity. I have my list beside me. I'm going to quit making excuses about my areas of immaturity and begin to tackle them one at a time. No one else can change *my life*. Each person needs to accept responsibility for who she is. If you feel a need for spiritual growth, I encourage you to start with this exercise.

Once we understand our own pathway toward maturity, we can reach out and lead our children along that road. I have a picture that helps me visualize the process. Each child is born in the "Valley Birthing Center." He arrives fully dependent, accepting no responsibility. Each day, each week, each month, each year he understands more of who he is, and inch by inch he pulls away from his mother until by age 18 he is hopefully nearing the top of the hill. As mothers we can greatly accelerate a child's maturing process or we can keep him on a leash with a stake driven and cemented in the valley of dependency.

The only way for children to become adults (isn't that our goal?) is to have time to climb this hill to independence, leaving dependence behind. This hill of evaluation causes them to ask many questions and rethink their position and opinion on each topic they face. By helping our children accept responsibility in more and more areas, we prepare them to be mature socially, emotionally, mentally, physically, and spiritually. Most important is the spiritual. The decisions they make in this area will affect all other areas, and will eventually determine their forever home!

10

To Work or Not to Work

Debbie struggles with her job all day, then struggles with her kids all evening and struggles with her husband before she gets ready for bed. She knows she is trying to juggle too many balls. The kids are getting out of hand and her husband doesn't understand. She is existing—not living.

Frances is committed to full-time mothering but often feels she accomplishes little in a day, and struggles with her concept of fulfillment.

Maureen just quit her job to stay home with her little David. She couldn't handle the emotional fatigue of handing her screaming child over to a sitter each morning. "I didn't have children to give them away," she says. "No amount of money is worth it."

Kelly wonders if maybe the money might be worth it. There are so many things they need, and her husband, a schoolteacher, will never make a high salary.

Lisa is determined to succeed in her career but feels stabbed in the heart when her mother says, "What a horrible price you are paying to have a career!"

Among Christian women, especially Christian mothers, the most sensitive and controversial topic to discuss is whether or not a mother should work outside the home. Not only is emotion generated, but sincere conviction is adamantly expressed by card-carriers from both arenas. Friendships can be scarred by sharing such deep convictions. Families can feel torn apart. Mothers-in-law can shatter communication with their daughters-in-law. I believe I have tried all the alternatives at various times. I have worked outside the home, doing a daily radio show and operating a dress shop. I've also worked at home teaching piano. And there have been periods of time when I didn't work at all in order to concentrate entirely on my family.

It is difficult to think clearly on this issue when the media influence so many of our choices. For most women, excluding some single parents, working or not working outside the home is simply a choice. The questions are:

- How do women go about making this choice?
- Who do they allow to influence them?
- What do they take into consideration?
- Years later, are they happy with the choices they made and the results that followed?
- When they choose to work, do they feel that the fulfillment and extra finances enhance the life of their family?
- Can women agree that circumstances dictate different choices for different women?

Let's try to sort out some of our beliefs, prejudices, convictions, and priorities in an attempt to help us mothers examine our options.

Advantages of Working Outside the Home

1. *Money.* It's the number one reason most women work. The added income provides added buying

power for the family. However, many women don't realize how much—or little—money they actually make. To find out your *real* earning power, begin with your gross income, then *subtract* the following:

- Taxes (including Social Security).
- The cost of child care.
- Expenses such as lunches out, a "more-appropriate" wardrobe, and a "more reliable" car.

Now take this amount and divide it by the number of hours you work to figure your *actual* profit per hour. This should help to clarify if working outside the home is as financially beneficial as you had assumed.

2. *Benefits.* Many women, realizing that the cost of working eats up their salary, work for the benefits alone. These can include pension, retirement, or investment plans, but most important—a medical and/or dental plan. A good health insurance package can mean a lot to a family. With two or three children each catching a few of the normal childhood diseases and ear infections plus a few cavities...you're broke! And that doesn't include the 2500 dollars (times the number of children you have) needed to outfit each child in braces. That kind of cash is hard to come by. A job that can cover a family's medical expenses is a significant advantage.

3. *Fulfillment.* Every woman knows how good it feels to be thanked, appreciated, admired, and respected. In the professional world, *you're somebody!* You accomplish important assignments each day, and these provide a feeling of worth.

As a mother, I have had whole days slip between my fingers when at dusk I felt like I had accomplished nothing. Feelings affect our self-confidence and productivity.

When my older girls were preschoolers, and I had been home full-time for a number of years, I decided to do a little substitute teaching. It lasted all of four days, but what a feeling! I awoke in the morning with a reason to dress up, put on my makeup, and got my day started briskly. I arrived at school as a *respected professional*. I had *power* over the 25 students before me. I commanded silence and they obeyed. I could read while they read (far deeper books than the fairy tales we were into at home). When recess came, they were gone and I had 15 minutes to sip coffee with my feet up. At home there was never an "off-duty" time. At the end of the day when I returned home I felt entitled to relax with my husband in the evening because we had both worked hard all day. Plus I felt fulfillment in the wonderful lessons I taught my students, the controlled classroom I maintained because of my consistent discipline, and the warm fuzzies I received as I reached out in love to some needy students during the day.

Having taught school full-time for four years, I recognize that not every day presents such a "high." But fulfillment and daily verbal strokes are an advantage to working outside the home.

4. *Public affirmation.* Years ago society raised its eyebrow at the mother who was employed outside the home, leaving a latchkey child to fend for himself. Not so today! The courageous career woman is applauded as hardworking, energetic, and committed to a cause.

5. *Broadened world view.* The work-world relationship with other adults provides an environment for intellectual stimulation, resulting in dinner conversation deeper than changing diapers and grocery lists.

Disadvantages of Working Outside the Home

1. *Time robbed from mothering.* Time is an intangible element that can make or break a marriage, a family, and our own emotional well-being. Time is sometimes divided into quality and quantity parts. Supposedly they are a trade-off—equal options. "Quality time" implies mother and child spending very little time together, but using this time to best advantage—focusing on the needs of the child and maximizing the minutes spent together. It sounds beautiful, but rarely accomplishes what it promises. "Quantity time" implies mother and child spending volumes of time together, but rarely tuning in to any needs or recognizing teachable moments. It's "putting in the time" in a halfhearted manner.

Neither option is adequate. As mothers we need to spend both quantity *and* quality time with our children—playing with them, providing an atmosphere of security, teaching them, disciplining them, molding them, directing them. Mothers who work outside the home rarely have time for both of these necessary elements. They feel robbed of their time for mothering. Many authorities say it is the children who are robbed, but that's only partly true, for a mother also has a need for this togetherness time. She has only a few years when her children are at the dependent age when they need her time so desperately. She needs to be around to catch those famous infant "firsts"—the first smile, the first rollover, the first step.

2. *Energy robbed from mothering.* Apart from the time element, mothers who work expend much of their day's energy at the job and come home quite spent. They're too tired to hear about the problems and squabbles their children experienced that day. They're too tired to consistently discipline their young

ones. They're too tired to properly investigate where an older one has spent his time after school. Overlooking areas of potential conflict is a coping technique. She knows that this is not the best method of mothering, but she only has so much energy.

3. *Guilt-producing stress and stress-producing guilt.* Maybe you're one of these supermoms who can meet every need within her household plus achieve great success in her professional field. Maybe you've developed some skill at juggling, as I have. But I haven't found anyone who can keep it up. Eventually stress takes its toll, and when it does, guilt finishes you off. In situations where full-time employment outside the home is an unnegotiable necessity, compromises must be worked out. You cannot be all things to all people. Christians who believe that no woman should ever work outside the home will make you feel guilty. As you try to be a full-time mother to impress your accusers while trying to succeed in your full-time career, you will suffer from stress. If you slow down a little to protect your sanity you will feel guilty because you're not all that you want to be in each role.

4. *No time for me.* We all need time for ourselves— to read, to meditate, to exercise, to socialize with a friend. If you work full-time, plus take care of your husband and children, plus have time for yourself, I don't know how you do it! One area always suffers. Some women work all day, then head to the health spa and exercise for an hour, then have coffee with a friend before coming home. Three or four nights a week the children have to fix whatever they can for supper, and if they're lucky they'll see their mother before they go to bed. On the other hand, if a woman works full-time, then races home to pour the rest of her life into her children, there is no time for her. She can't do this for long without damage to her health.

In cases where a single mother must work full-time and her children also need every possible hour of her evenings, she should schedule fun and meaningful lunch hours for herself. Treat yourself to a quiet time or an hour of shopping. You should also schedule one evening out a week—for you. That will help you devote the rest of your time to teaching your children and enjoying their company.

5. *Babysitter problems.* Child care is probably the number one concern for working mothers. It is a recurrent problem because no substitute commits to your child for life. Mothers often find themselves seeking new sitters, and it's tough to find one who has your values and priorities.

A very real problem of child care arises during the ordeal of childhood illnesses and middle-of-the-day crises. What is a mother to do? Lie to her employer and say that *she* is sick? Let someone else take care of her child, knowing that the child wants and needs his mother?

Sometimes a husband's schedule is flexible and he can take some turns with the sick child. A single mother does not have this option. I believe she must work out a solution with her employer, for she must be home with her children during these critical times. She may need to use up her sick days, or take some days without pay—even though money is tight—or take work home if the boss will allow it.

Advantages of Full-Time Mothering

1. *Modeling your priorities.* All of us would no doubt agree that our husbands come first, then our children, and then the outside world or our careers. The mother who purposefully stays at home to care for her family takes a public stand about her priorities. She is devoting

this segment of her life to caring for her husband and children. She is "modeling" her priority. Titus 2:4,5 advises older women to "encourage the young women to love their husbands, to love their children, to be sensible, pure, *workers at home*, kind, being subject to their own husbands, that the word of God may not be dishonored."

2. *Time and energy to accomplish your mothering goals.* During her pregnancy and the early days of her baby's life, every mother has dreams and goals for her child. She plans to be the best mother she can be. The woman who has a full 24 hours a day available has a major advantage over the working mother in rearing her child according to her dreams. Of course, that advantage can be wasted, as we'll see in the list of disadvantages.

3. *Time for hobbies, friends, and you.* The years I worked in various professional arenas provided fulfillment, but no spare time. Because I was a hardworking, determined mother, I kept my children's schedule as number one priority. I was always home before they arrived home from school, and I managed to continue my volunteer activities at their school. I did everything on the job description to be a good mother. I also completed every requirement to succeed in my professional career as a musician, clothing store owner, or radio show host. All parties seemed happy and satisfied—except me. There was no leisure time, except a few hurried coffee visits with my friends. There was even less time for me to appreciate my life, which was flying by quickly. I felt cheated.

Our children are only young once. We are only young mothers once. We need to be reminded to "stop and smell the flowers." The days are flying by—one day at a time, never to be relived. Our children age, and so do we.

4. *Upgrading quality of family living (other than financially).* As a mother at home most of the day, I have time to cook more nutritiously, shop more economically, and live more conservatively. This is an advantage when I consider the health of my family. When I work outside the home we eat more meals in restaurants, which is a disadvantage financially *and* nutritionally.

As a mother at home most of the day, I can take care of many family needs that otherwise might require hired help—mending, cleaning, child care, lawn and garden maintenance, etc. I can also provide a loving, relaxed atmosphere for my husband and children to return to at the end of their day, because I have time to relax myself and prepare the home for their return. The word "home" connotes love, acceptance, respect, and appreciation in a cozy, comfortable environment suitable to the particular needs of the individuals who live there. "Home" implies a person's favorite chair, favorite books, games, snacks—and for me, my piano. Home is where you love and are loved. A mother at home has time to tune in to the needs of her family and decorate and set the atmosphere to enhance her loved ones' lives.

5. *Availability for open communication.* "Availability" is probably the key word when it comes to full-time mothering. "Availability" is a sacrificial exercise but one that boasts long-term rewards. Being available is a key to open communication. Preschoolers and mothers chatter back and forth, on and off, all day long. With school-age children, the chatter begins before school and picks up the minute they walk in the door after school. Before school is an important time because we can set the mood for the child's day. Even when I have had a job, the earliest I have ever gone in to work is ten in the morning. I'm thankful

for this because I could calmly focus on the needs of my family in the morning, sending them off calm and confident of my love and support. Once I was alone in the house, I could prepare myself for the day. This may be an ideal situation, but one that you might want to pursue.

Presently, I find the immediate after-school sharing to be most beneficial. Each of my girls arrives home with an appetite and stories to tell. We have a snack at the kitchen table while they tell me about the day. I have come to realize how very important this time of communication is. I have always been home when my girls came home from school, but for a number of years I was in the living room teaching piano. They would come in the door, give me a kiss, and find a snack laid out for them. I would also remind them, "Shhh! Be quiet." The interpretation was: "You can't talk to me now. I'm doing something more important. Go play and I'll hear your stories at dinnertime." By dinner the girls had either lost their enthusiasm or forgotten what they had wanted to tell me, or else their minds were on other things—like a television program they had watched because I was busy and they were bored. As much as I love to teach piano, I have not taught for several years because it occupies me at the time my children need me. The benefit of daily open communication is worth the cost.

Disadvantages of Full-time Mothering

1. *Sticking to a tight budget.* All moderate-income families in America need to establish a budget that takes care of their needs within the monies they receive each month. No one feels the pinch more than the full-time mother. There is no extra income. There is no fun money to play with. Depending on her

husband's income, she often needs to be frugal. She needs to be a good and trustworthy manager, not a "splurger." Lunches out at sophisticated restaurants and hired housecleaners and babysitters are not part of her economic structure. She can feel strapped financially, tied to her house and kids, and can develop a negative, bitter attitude that could wipe out all the good she has accomplished by staying home full-time. Most discontented homemakers zero in on the negatives. There are various names for these kinds of women:

> "It is better to live in a corner of the roof than in a house shared with a contentious woman" (Proverbs 25:24).

> "The contentions of a wife are a constant dripping" (Proverbs 19:13).

2. *Feeling low self-esteem.* To feel our lives are worthwhile means to live with dignity, to be appreciated, and to give and receive love. If one or more of the above areas is injured and our self-respect drops, we experience a great disadvantage with full-time mothering. Our present-day society does not respect the role of mother as much as it should. In this day it takes guts to stay at home. It is difficult to willingly and happily give up an exciting career to give our children the best, knowing that some people are saying, "It's such a waste." If we focus on what society is saying, tuning in to women's libbers, we begin to doubt our commitment, our priorities, and peace in God's plan. I do believe in woman as being equal before God. I do believe in equal pay for equal work. But that should not turn us away from God's plan for our lives. When we are home full-time it can be difficult to keep things in perspective. It is imperative that we believe what we are doing is

significant. Being a productive full-time housewife is no little feat. It is also healthy to remember that even amid whatever exciting career we may have had before, we experienced days that were frustrating and boring.

3. *Unhappy-homemaker or pious-martyr attitude.* Attitude seems to make the difference in much of life, and attitude is the hardest thing to change—without God's help. Full-time homemakers may be unhappy because they feel they are wasting their life. Without a purpose and a plan, a woman in the home 24 hours a day does not necessarily achieve admirable goals. She may accomplish household tasks while inside she slowly disintegrates due to an unhappy spirit or negative thinking.

An opposite is not always a positive attitude. It may be a superior, pious, "better than thou" attitude, or a "living sacrifice" martyr attitude. Some full-time homemakers become extremely judgmental. They criticize any working mother no matter what the circumstances, and react unsympathetically to any woman who does not torture herself with the same daily tasks that weigh down this unhappy home-maker.

The Scriptures teach us to not have critical spirits, but to show love to one another. The pious martyr has gone beyond the "Martha example" and proclaimed herself the only proper full-time homemaker worthy of a pity-party while the rest of the frivolous busy-bodies live in sin. In Matthew 7:1 Jesus talks about motives and right responses: "Do not judge lest you be judged."

Other Observations

- Most fights in marriages and within families are over money. Dual-income couples

fight more often than single-income families.

- Dual-income couples tend to focus on economic success, thereby producing stress that affects other important areas of life.
- Some wives admit they are employed because they are not satisfied with their husband's salary. This dissatisfaction insinuates that the husband is somewhat of a failure. This causes self-doubt in the husband and begins to break down the marriage relationship.
- Christian society often judges a husband for allowing his wife to work, putting increased stress on the marriage relationship. The wife can feel the church is frowning at her for having a professional career, and this creates tension and stress within her family at home and her church family.
- The world often judges a woman's worth by her profession. This gauge of personal worth interprets a full-time mother as lazy, with no potential and low intelligence. This is, of course, a false gauge of personal worth—our worth is not found in a particular profession but in the knowledge that we are doing with our lives what God would have us do.
- As mothers, and as a society, we have become so selfish that we can rationalize anything for the sake of self-fulfillment.

Unjust Justice?

A man has a relatively simple game plan when he is born. He grows up, gets a job, and works (builds his career) for the rest of his life. He may have difficult changes in his career, but he never has to evaluate

"Should I be working or should I not?" His existence requires that he work.

> "You shall work six days, but on the seventh day you shall rest; even during plowing time and harvest you shall rest" (Exodus 34:21).

Even before the first sin in the garden of Eden, God assigned the first man work:

> "The Lord God took the man and put him into the garden of Eden to cultivate it and keep it" (Genesis 2:15).

A woman has a different job description:

> "To the woman He said, 'I will greatly multiply your pain in childbirth; in pain you shall bring forth children. Yet your desire shall be for your husband, and he shall rule over you' " (Genesis 3:16).

Only because of sin was there conflict between husband and wife. Only because of sin was childbirth a great discomfort.

A woman's job description can be studied throughout the Bible, but Proverbs 31 pretty well sums up the "perfect woman." We can study this job description and be challenged by the opportunities available to us.

Alternatives

1. *Work full-time outside the home.* I believe this decision needs to be made in accordance with the age of your children, the desire of your husband, and your financial need. Apart from absolute financial *need* (not

financial *desire*), I personally believe that a mother with preschoolers should waive her right to work outside the home. She has given birth to these children and should accept the responsibility to rear them. Yes, this is a sacrifice. Better yet, it is a commitment and a high calling, for it is God who has written her job description.

Once all her children are in school, I believe that a woman still needs to evaluate whether she should work outside the home or not. She is still responsible for preparing the children for school in the morning and seeing that they use the after-school hours to good advantage. Also, she should consider her energy level and what she feels she can handle in the work world while remaining a good mother.

2. *Work part-time outside the home.* Once her children are all in school, a woman might consider this option as a perfect solution, providing a challenge for her while maintaining a home that meets the needs of her family. Again, she must consider the hours required, how this will affect her family, and her energy level.

3. *Work professionally within the home.* This is an option that may be just the answer, or just the headache that could ruin the atmosphere in your home. What hours of the day would be needed to run this business? What rooms of the house would be used? What family members would be affected by the undertaking?

If you run a day-care center for children, you need to set up rules as to what rooms in your home are out-of-bounds. My neighbor, Karen, kept her living room perfect by reserving it for her own personal guests and not for the children she babysat. In Karen's case, she did a great job with the kids, and she needed the extra income her work generated. But she was also aware that her children sometimes felt they lacked the extra attention they deserved when they came home from school.

The many years I taught piano affected not only my children, but my husband. He would arrive home from work ready for peace and solitude, only to be greeted by parents of my piano students waiting for a lesson to be completed. They would visit with Paul while waiting siblings used our bathroom or asked for glasses of water. Paul didn't mind visiting with these friendly parents, but they didn't realize this was a night-after-night occurrence, and Paul felt like he didn't have a home to come home to.

Much evaluation and sensitivity is necessary to determine if an at-home occupation can work for you. If you can control your hours and set protective guidelines to preserve your privacy, this could still be your best option.

4. *Don't work while you have children living at home.* If you can afford this option, be thankful. Do not take for granted this wonderful luxury. Yes, it is a luxury— if you can truly afford it in this day of economic inflation. If you can and do choose to stay at home, use the time to educate your children and enjoy these fun years. Let me also caution you to not make other mothers feel badly if they cannot afford what you can afford. God has blessed you. Be gracious about your blessing.

Another group of women may decide to not work while they have children living at home, but sacrifice materially in order to do this. This is the group of mothers I salute the most. These women are bold enough and care enough about responsibly rearing their children that they deny themselves things like a nicer house, a second car, eating out, and new clothes. Let me offer a word of caution to these full-time mothers. You have made a mature decision to do without in order to be home with your children. Don't spend your days complaining about what you don't have. Your children aren't impressed and your friends will slowly tire of the whining and will drift away. Be positive in the decision you make and positive in how you live it out. God will honor you, and other people will be blessed through you and your family.

5. *"A little of each" free-lance living.* The Proverbs 31 woman definitely takes care of her family's needs—providing them beautiful clothing, feeding them nutritionally, and causing her husband and children to praise her. But look at all the other things she does! This is not to minimize the mother who can only cope with running her household effectively. Each woman is created unique, with a different capacity for work. I relate to the Proverbs 31 lady. Some of my friends get tired just watching me. Goals and projects rev my engine! But even my own accomplishments make me look lazy when compared with the Proverbs 31 lady. She is *always* doing good. She works with her hands weaving wool and flax. She brings choice foods to her family.

I don't like to read verse 15, where she gets up so early in the morning. But I *love* reading the end of that verse, where it talks about her maidens (servants). Now we're talking! If you can afford it, don't feel guilty about hiring another woman to clean your house. It can free you to accomplish other more important tasks.

The Proverbs 31 woman was an efficient lady, but she also helped people. She gave to the poor and spoke wisdom with kindness. She had a career and worked very hard at it (verses 16-18). She had a business on the side (verse 24). She had a wonderful reputation and was known for her integrity (verse 31). What I notice most about her was that she was a *confident woman.*

Why was she confident? Because she had made her choices and worked hard while keeping her priorities in line with God's design for her. She did what she believed God wanted her to do and therefore felt peace and satisfaction.

We each have different abilities and capabilities. We each have different financial situations. We each have children at different ages. Some are single parents. Others are married to men who are handicapped or bedridden and can't support the family. Some should be home rearing their children but are out in the workplace because of greed. Others are wasting time and neglecting their children even when they are home. Let's seek God's help and direction in determining where we should spend our time and energy. God will richly bless us for it.

> "Charm is deceitful and beauty is vain, but a woman who fears the Lord, she shall be praised" (Proverbs 31:30).

11

More Than Just a Mother

Amid screaming children, messy kitchens, and the smell of soiled diapers it is very easy for young mothers to turn off the learning and thinking parts of their brains. With "no time" to read books, skim newspapers, or enjoy the arts, even the study of God's Word becomes a chore.

To be born a woman is a most wonderful yet most confusing role, most beautiful yet most controversial, most creative yet seemingly contradictory. Motherhood is an important calling, but *not* the only reason for our existence. You know by now that I am a firm believer in motherhood and acknowledge its priority in my life.

Some women consider being born a woman a negative, a jail sentence, a verification that slavery has not yet been abolished. These women have not caught God's vision for us.

> "There is neither Jew nor Greek, there is neither slave nor free man, there is neither male nor female; for you are all one in Christ Jesus" (Galatians 3:28).

As women, we must realistically face ourselves. We are not just good "appliances" that perform a variety of functions. Yes, we have most challenging job descriptions assigned us at birth. These are not negatives. Neither are these all positives. They simply describe what we do. We need to recognize our worth as people, then evaluate what we feel called to accomplish. This becomes the source of our dreams, and our dreams lead us to make choices.

> "Where there is no vision [dream/goals], the people are unrestrained" (Proverbs 29:18).

Let's step back and look once more at God's big picture and see the choices we have as women.

Born a Woman

The *only* area in our life where we have absolutely no choice is in our sex. We are women. God chose or predestined us to be female.

> "Thou didst weave me in my mother's womb. I will give thanks to Thee, for I am fearfully and wonderfully made; wonderful are Thy works, and my soul knows it very well. My frame was not hidden from Thee when I was made in secret, and skillfully wrought in the depths of the earth. Thine eyes have seen my unformed substance; and in Thy book they were all written, the days that were ordained for me, when as yet there was not one of them" (Psalm 139:13-16).

If we really believe that, let's trust that God made His perfect choice in creating us female. He chose us to have blue eyes or brown eyes, to have blonde hair or red hair, to be five-foot-nine or four-foot-eleven, to be artistic or athletic. Each of us is a custom design, with exact specifications for our purpose on earth. We begin to understand ourselves by acknowledging that God is God and accepting His design for us.

Reborn a Christian

Once we step beyond the classification of female, we all begin to differ. We have an incredible array of choices. But one choice stands above them all: the one concerning God and where He rates on our priority list. The most important choice I have ever made is to become a born-again Christian. Pleasing God is my highest calling. Spending time reading His Word and talking to Him is my most important time each day. That's why I carve out some quiet time to follow this command:

"Be still and know that I am God" (Psalm 46:10 KJV).

Communion with God has enriched my life more than anything else. These moments when God and I are whispering to each other are the highlights of my day. In the stillness, God has put thoughts in my head, telling me exactly what He wants me to do. He has put a peace in my heart, assuring me of His care and protection.

If you are a mother who has not taken time to know God in this intimate way, I pray that you will stop right now and ask Jesus into your life. This will affect the rest of your life more than anything else. If you are longing for inner strength, peace, purpose, and direction, I invite you to pray this prayer:

Dear God,
You are so great, and I am so needy. I

confess to You that I have done many wrong
things in my life, the worst being my neglecting You. I ask You to forgive my sins. Thank
You for sending Your Son, Jesus, to die on the
cross for me. Thank You that He rose from
the dead that I might be saved from eternal
death and live forever with You in heaven.
Thank You, Holy Spirit, for coming into my
life, to help me from within. I love You,
Father, Son, and Holy Spirit. By faith, through
this prayer, I step into your Christian family.
I pray to You in Jesus' name. Amen.

If you have just prayed this prayer, please write me.
I am thrilled for you, and the angels in heaven are
rejoicing at this moment. You have just made the most
important choice of your lifetime.

Becoming a Wife

Here's another choice that affects the rest of our lives.
If we choose to be a wife, we commit ourselves to being
a lover, a loyal friend, and a supporter to another
human being for the duration of his life. Once we have
made this commitment, we need to live out our promise! Barring immorality or harmful abuse, we must
work to maintain a loving commitment to our husband, respecting and honoring him.

No marriage is a continual honeymoon. As an old
pastor-friend explained, "Sometimes the tide's in—
sometimes it's out." We all experience romantic times
of deep love and exciting sharing. We also experience
times of stress, hurt, and disappointment—a "tide's
out" relationship. The word to remember is *commitment*. We chose to be a wife, and God tells us that our
relationship with our spouse is second only to our

relationship with God. Yes, being a wife even takes precedence over being a mother.

This priority poses a conflict for many young mothers. They find it difficult to leave their child with a babysitter in order to enjoy an evening out or a weekend away with their husband. They find it difficult to set aside time to show affection to their husbands because they're showering love on their little infant day and night. We all need a little reminder: We are responsible for our children's welfare and happiness, but even more important is for us to make our man happy.

Paul and I try to get away alone one weekend every spring and every fall. We farm the kids out to friends. (Develop some friendships with people who will occasionally swap weekend babysitting with you. You take their kids for a few days and then they take yours.) We drive a couple of hours to a quaint hotel in a nearby city. We enjoy long candlelight dinners, walks in the moonlight, lunches at outside cafes, and lots of hugging and laughing. We spend time reading the Bible together and praying on our knees. We also set aside a few hours on the second day to evaluate. We ask each other questions like:

- Are you happy with how your life is right now?
- Are we accomplishing our goals for this year?
- How are the children coming along?
- Do you think Melanie is overinvolved at school? Should we slow her down some?
- Should Cheryl continue violin through junior high?
- Are we giving Deanna enough chores to do around the house?

- How's our love life?
- Is Paul fulfilled in his job? Does he still believe he's where God wants him to be?
- Am I content with my activities?
- Are we challenged by the goals we've committed ourselves to?
- What is the greatest thing in our life right now?
- What is the worst area in our life right now?
- What should we change?

From our evaluation we list changes we want to make and set some new goals. Then we spend some time in prayer, committing the next six months to God. Every time we have done this we have enjoyed the beauty of talking about what really counts in life. People never plan to live a mediocre life; it just happens because they don't plan anything else. *We don't want this to happen to us, so we plan!*

As a wife, I don't want to just exist in a marriage. I don't want a good marriage; I want a *great* marriage. This will only happen as Paul and I work together, and as I recognize that our marriage is second in importance only to our commitment to God.

Motherhood

Motherhood is the role I am working hard at now while I have children living in my home. The importance of my influence on them will affect the world today and for generations to come. Motherhood is a career I take seriously. My children are more important to me than anything else in the world, after God and Paul. Children need to know how valuable they are, that we love them unconditionally, and that we care for them sacrificially. *They also need to know that they are not number one in our lives.* They should see us put our husband's needs ahead of theirs. They will not consider this depriving them, but rather providing for their security.

One method I use to organize my mothering is a trusty notebook. For simplicity I use standard 8½ x 5½ paper (3 holes) and cover for all of my notebooks. This makes it easy to "transfer files" when necessary. Here are a few of my notebooks:

- Personal Notebook
- Family Council Notebook
- Bible Study Notes
- Address and Phone Numbers
- Favorite Recipes

You may prefer *one* notebook with many chapters (dividers). My trusty personal notebook (in a classy, more expensive cover) is my life on paper. It contains such things as prayer lists and my journal. I've already told you about our Family Council Notebook; it has a country-print quilted fabric cover. My Bible Study Notebook contains all the sermon notes and personal Bible study notes which I transfer out of my personal notebook. (Just like my purse, I need to clean it out from time to time.) It's ready to use for my speaking engagements or leading a ladies' study.

In my Personal Notebook I keep a chapter on each person in the family. For Paul, I write down special prayer requests for him and keep track of things I want to discuss with him.

For each of my girls, I write down specific goals and prayers. I title the chapter by their name. After their name I write their birthdate, followed by an equation such as 18 - 12 = 6. This represents the 18 probable years that my child will be under my teaching minus her current age, equalling the number of years I have left to accomplish my goals as a mother.

My goals for each child include spiritual, mental, physical, and social goals, plus areas of talent that need to be developed, areas of her personality that need to be developed, manners she needs to work on, and so on. I rank the goals in order of importance and use this list as a prayer list. Every six to twelve months I evaluate our progress and make any necessary readjustments. This gives me a visible direction—a chartable course—for my mothering. I don't want to wander aimlessly from year to year, then feel frustrated or disgusted that my child didn't grow up the way I wanted her to. I don't want my child to reach age 18 with me thinking "I always meant to tell her to eat with her mouth closed!"

With goals clearly defined day by day, in "teachable moments" I teach the skills and encourage the positive attitudes that I believe are important.

Let's draw up a sample list of goals for a three-year-old boy:

1. SPIRITUAL	• Each day tell Billy that Jesus loves him.
	• Say John 3:16 to him every day (or whatever verse you choose).
2. MENTAL	• Read two books to him every day.
	• Say the alphabet to him every day.
	• Talk about colors during lunch hour.
3. PHYSICAL	• Play ball at least once a week.
	• Go for a walk three times a week.

4. SOCIAL
- Have a friend over one afternoon each week (teach "sharing" and "together" games).
- Take Billy to children's Bible class one morning a week while I go to Bible Study Fellowship.

5. TALENTS
- Let Billy draw one picture a week for me to put on my refrigerator.
- Play records of various kinds of music, and sing along.

6. PERSONALITY
- Laugh at funny stories and let him tell Daddy stories when he comes home.

7. MANNERS
- Practice "Please" and "Thank you" this year!

If you're not a visual person and hate keeping notebooks or making lists, then discuss some goals with your husband or a close friend. Then begin to work on them. Having someone pray for you and check up on you is a great help.

If you're a good listener, I would encourage you to grow under the teaching of a man of God who has strengthened and encouraged me as a mother. I have only met him on one occasion, but I listen to him every day. Dr. James Dobson's radio program "Focus on the Family" has, in my opinion, done more to encourage Christian women and mothers than any other program I know of in America. I want to publicly thank Dr. Dobson for the ministry he has had in my life.

Friendships

Our society has finally rediscovered the importance of friendships. Today we frequently hear about networking and support groups. We do need each other!

As a mother, allow yourself some loving, supportive friends. Forego "baby talk" and indulge in stimulating conversation, sharing knowledge and encouraging each other. Remember that a friend is a gift you give yourself.

For a number of years the only time I could meet with friends was early in the morning. For several years I met Sandy at the corner at 6 A.M. for a walk and talk. Our sharing and caring and praying was a stimulating way to start our day. Once a week Eunie, Jeannie, Karen, Sue, and I would meet at 6 A.M. at Denny's. We would eat breakfast, share our prayer requests, encourage each other in our goals for the week, and promise to pray throughout the week for each other. A support group like this meeting for just one to one-and-a-half hours a week can change your attitude and your effectiveness.

Ministry

God will allow us to touch people's lives and witness through the various roles He gives us. Just as I believe that every Christian should tithe his or her money, I believe that every Christian should tithe his or her time. Our local church needs our participation, and we need to be involved in ministry. While we are tied down with young children, our tasks might be small. That's okay. But we do need to do something for the Lord. Notice that I said "something"—not everything! Every time the phone rings it isn't the Lord calling. Jean Johnson shared this gem with me years ago, and it has helped me say no to tasks that aren't right for me: Don't let people tell you how to spend your time—let God.

Career

Whether our career is an ongoing occupation, or we're working part-time, or we're taking time out to rear our children, let's not let our career climb any higher on our priority list than it should. "Now" is not the perfect time to do everything. Our worth is not in what we do, but in who we are.

If your career is in its proper priority, then achieving and excelling is admirable. If you have goals that have sat on the shelf for years, continue to pray and wait for God's timing. When your children are reared and your husband has agreed with your goals, go for it. If you do not take care of your husband's and children's needs first, then I do not believe that God will honor your career.

I was inspired the other day as I read the Dear Abby column: A 36-year-old college dropout had a lifelong ambition to become a doctor. Her children were all in school and her husband was encouraging her. But she was hesitating because she would be 43 years old before she completed the necessary seven years of study. Abby's reply was to question how old she thought she would be in seven years if she didn't study to be a doctor! *It's never too late if you don't want it to be.*

You may not feel God calling you to be a doctor, but you have many productive years ahead that can be used in a very effective way. Many women pick up their career at age 40 and build it until they're in their sixties. When you are 22 or 28 or 31, you think your kids will never be out of the diaper stage and you'll never get all your children into school and you'll never be able to have time to do what you'd like to do. When I was 34, I thought I'd never reach 35 and get Deanna into school all day. Well, that day did arrive. Deanna went to school. I cried. Now that I had all those hours alone during the day, after 12 years of 24-hours-a-day duty, I wasn't sure what I wanted to do.

Dr. Kay Kuzma challenges women in an article "Making Your Dreams Come True" (*Family Life Today* magazine, January 1986) to clarify and write down their dreams. She suggests that we truthfully answer this question: "If there were no barriers, what would you really like to do in life?" Many people stumble through life feeling unfulfilled because they've never taken the time to determine what they'd *really* like to do. About the time they're ready for the shelf, you hear them finish the sentence, "You know, if I could live my life over again, I'd really like to _____."

Dr. Kuzma suggests that you list your interests and talents, and analyze your spiritual gifts (Romans 12 and 1 Corinthians 12). Then write down your dreams—what desires God has put in your heart, what you feel He is calling you to do. Then share your dream with a supportive friend, and take the first step!

Hobbies

A hobby is a project that you absolutely *love* to do. Sometimes a hobby involves a skill that ties in with your profession. My music is a hobby—I love it for my own enjoyment—but it is also my profession. Your artistic ability might be a hobby, but you can also sell your creations. Some hobbies are just for fun and later become valuable (such as collections). Other hobbies are just for laughs—and laughing is an important part of living!

You choose:

- Reading
- Thinking

- Writing
- Studying
- Furthering your education
- Learning to play a musical instrument
- Singing (possibly with your child)
- Exercising

This is your life. Don't waste it. Do the things that *you* want to do. Develop the gifts that you believe you have.

- Enjoy your life.
- Love people.
- Strive to feed your mind.
- Desire to love who you are.
- Be the best you can be.
- Be natural. Be yourself.

Relaxation, Recreation, and Restoration

Don't work all the time. God also wants us to rest. He wants us to appreciate His creation. He wants us to welcome the gifts He gives us. As the most loving father in the universe, God delights in providing for us physically, mentally, emotionally, and spiritually. Relax in His love.

> "Just as a father has compassion on his children, so the Lord has compassion on those who fear Him" (Psalm 103:13).

A Will

You can tell I'm nearing the end of this book. "Ends" are inevitable on this earth. As in all other areas, planning and ordering our end is honoring to God.

As a mother, you need a will to legally outline your wishes for your children if you should pass away before they reach adulthood. Actually *every* adult needs a will to orderly complete his or her steward-ship responsibility on earth. As difficult as this might seem, don't neglect this important responsibility.

Estate-planning provides peace of mind. Every mother prays that she will be able to rear her own children and then live to enjoy her grandchildren. I pray that God will give us this desire of our hearts. But as responsible parents we should still complete a legal will so that *we*, not the government, will choose who will finish raising our children and how they should be educated in our absence. A reasonable insurance policy should take care of the needed expenses. Before you make an appointment with a lawyer, prayerfully choose guardians—a Christian rela-tive or family—who would rear your children closest to your values. Meet with your chosen couple and ask their permission. On your will you might also list a second choice.

When making a will, you might like to leave a final testimony or letter to your loved ones. This letter could express your hopes, dreams, and prayers for your children. Thank the Lord if they never need to read it, and keep it as a prayer reminder for your children's lives and as a reminder of the privilege that each day with them is.

The Real Me

You may know me as Melanie, Cheryl, and Deanna's mother. Others know me as Paul's wife. For years I was recognized as Doug and Sue's daughter. Then I became Bannatyne School's music teacher. In the music world I am known as a keyboard player. At home I am a cook and laundry woman. None of these roles is exclusively me, nor are your roles you.

Motherhood is the focus of my book and the focus of my life right now. But motherhood is not my total identity.

Being cautious not to become selfish in a "me" society, let me still encourage you to take good care of yourself amid your mothering. Take time for lunch out with a friend. Sign up for a night course that will expand your mind or skills. Take mini "me-breaks" during your day. Enjoy a leisurely bubble bath with a book and a Coke (maybe not even a diet one!). In the middle of the afternoon when the kids are sleeping, make a fire just for you to relax by. Or make a quiet, romantic dinner for you and your husband to enjoy after the kids are in bed.

Keep up with fashion. Read new magazines. Stay involved. If you have preschoolers, find another mother who will exchange babysitting days with you. That way each of you can have some time off. It's amazing how a morning out or lunch out once a week can work wonders in putting your life into perspective. (Going grocery shopping, in my opinion, does not constitute a morning out.) Some days you may want to do nothing more than browse. This can be therapeutic. In this day and age of achieving, we need to be reminded that it is okay to relax. Don't feel guilty if you need a little time away from home.

Me and My Life

Motherhood is so wonderful . . . most of the time. If only we could stand back and see the whole picture, we would discover that it's only 20 or 30 years out of our life. True, once a mother, always a mother, but the endurance test comes only at the beginning. For years I thought, "Will I ever go to the bathroom without someone coming to sit on the edge of the tub for a chat? Will I ever take a bath without a toddler trying to climb in?" The sad answer is—yes. The days fly by quicker than we realize, never to be relived.

Suppose you were given 27,375 dollars today to buy yourself whatever you wanted. Each woman reading this would spend her money differently. She would evaluate her preferences and options, then make her choice. Once the money was spent, she would enjoy what she bought. Hopefully years later she would still be happy with the choice she made.

Now let's take the 27,375 dollars and convert it to something far more valuable. It starts with a "D." Diamonds, you say? No, more valuable than diamonds. DAYS! 365 days a year times 75 years equals 27,375. What a gift! How are you going to spend it? And how will you counsel your children to spend their inheritance?

> "O God, Thou hast taught me from my youth, and I still declare Thy wondrous deeds. And even when I am old and gray, O God, do not forsake me, until I declare Thy strength to this generation, Thy power to all who are to come" (Psalm 71:17,18).

God's Blessings on Your Mothering

I pray that you will be encouraged in your mothering, that you will be challenged in your own life, and that you will spend each day climbing the hill of responsibility, leading your children up the path toward maturity and forever pointing them to their heavenly Father, who loves them even more than you do.

Try to look beyond the tasks of each day to the future fruit of your labor. My final prayer for you is that you will be faithful in your *sowing*, relying on God for strength and wisdom. Then trust God with the results, patiently waiting for the day when...

"Her children rise up and bless her" (Proverbs 31:28).

Bibliography

CHAPTER 1

Barber, Cyril and Aldyth. *You Can Have a Happy Marriage*. Grand Rapids, MI: Kregel Publications, 1984.

Barber, Cyril and Aldyth. *Your Marriage Has Real Possibilities*. San Bernardino, CA: Here's Life Publishers, 1981.

Coble, Betty J. *Woman—Aware & Choosing*. Nashville, TN: Broadman Press, 1975.

Leman, Dr. Kevin. *The Birth Order Book*. Old Tappan, NJ: Fleming H. Revell, 1983.

Peterson, Evelyn R. and J. Allan. *For Women Only*. Wheaton, IL: Tyndale House, 1974.

Wright, H. Norman. *Communication: Key to Your Marriage*. Glendale, CA: Regal Books, 1979.

CHAPTER 2

Baker, Pat. *I Now Pronounce You Parent*. Grand Rapids, MI: Baker Book House, 1983.

Koop, C. Everett. *The Right to Live: the Right to Die*. Wheaton, IL: Tyndale House, 1976.

La Leche League International. *The Womanly Art of Breastfeeding*. 1963.

Messenger, Maire. *The Breastfeeding Book*. New York, NY: Van Nostrand Reinhold, 1982.

Young, Curt. *The Least of These*. Chicago, IL: Moody Press, 1984.

CHAPTER 3

Briscoe, Jill. *Fight for the Family*. Grand Rapids, MI: Zondervan, 1981.

Butterworth, Bill. *Peanut Butter Families Stick Together*. Old Tappan, NJ: Fleming H. Revell, 1973.

Christenson, Evelyn. *What Happens When Women Pray*. Wheaton, IL: Victor Books, 1975.

Felton, Sandra. *The Messies Manual*. Old Tappan, NJ: Fleming H. Revell, 1984.

Morgan, Marabel. *The Total Woman*. Old Tappan, NJ: Fleming H. Revell, 1973.

Ortlund, Anne. *The Disciplines of the Beautiful Woman*. Waco, TX: Word Books, 1977.

Wheeler, Bonnie. *The Hurrier I Go*. Ventura, CA: Regal Books, 1985.

Young, Pam and Jones, Peggy. *Sidetracked Home Executives*. New York, NY: Warner Books, 1981.

CHAPTER 4

Barber, Cyril and Strauss, Gary. *The Effective Parent*. San Bernardino, CA: Here's Life Publishers, 1980.

Dobson, James. *Dare to Discipline*. Wheaton, IL: Tyndale House, 1970.

Dobson, James. *Hide or Seek*. Old Tappan, NJ: Fleming H. Revell, 1974.

Leman, Dr. Kevin. *Making Children Mind, Without Losing Yours*. Old Tappan, NJ: Fleming H. Revell, 1984.

Smith, Joyce Marie. *Becoming the Parent Your Child Needs*. Wheaton, IL: Tyndale House, 1980.

Chapter 5

Lewis, Paul. *40 Ways to Teach Your Child Values*. Wheaton, IL: Tyndale House, 1985.

Meier, Paul D. *Christian Child Rearing and Personality Development*. Grand Rapids, MI: Baker Book House, 1977.

Owen, Pat H. *The Idea Book for Mothers*. Wheaton, IL: Tyndale House, 1981.

Powell, John. *Why Am I Afraid to Love?* Niles, IL: Argus Communications, 1972.

CHAPTER 6

Frank, Marge and Linton, Nancy. *Better, Better Body Book*. Grand Rapids, MI: Pyranee Books, 1985.

Heitritter, Lynn. *Little Ones*. Young America, MN: Little Ones Books, 1983.

Howe, Mary. "Kids and Exercise" in *Working Mother*, April 1985.

Kamen, Betty and Kamen, Si. *Kids Are What They Eat*. New York, NY: Arco Publishing, Inc., 1983.

Lansky, Vicki. *Getting Your Baby to Sleep & Back to Sleep.* New York, NY: Bantam Books, 1985.

Larson, Bruce. *There's a Lot More to Health Than Not Being Sick.* Waco, TX: Word Books, 1981.

Katz, William. *Protecting Your Children From Sexual Assault.* Toronto, Canada: Little Ones Books, 1983.

Natow, Annette and Heslin, JoAnn. *No-Nonsense Nutrition for Kids.* New York, NY: Pocket Books, 1986.

Schaeffer, Edith. *What Is a Family?* Old Tappan, NJ: Fleming H. Revell, 1975.

Tompkins, Iverna and Harrell, Irene B. *How to Live With Kids and Enjoy It.* Plainfield, NJ: Logos, 1977.

Townsend, Anne. *Marvelous Me.* San Diego, CA: Lion Publishing Corporation, 1984.

Ziglar, Zig. *Raising Positive Kids in a Negative World.* Nashville, TN: Thomas Nelson, 1985.

CHAPTER 7

Gorder, Cheryl. *Home Schools: An Alternative.* Columbus, OH: Blue Bird Publishing, 1985.

Hendricks, Howard G. *Heaven Help the Home!* Wheaton, IL: Victor Books, 1974.

Moore, Raymond S. *Home-Spun Schools: Teaching Children at Home.* Waco, TX: Word Books, 1982.

Moore, Raymond and Moore, Dorothy. *Home Grown Kids.* Waco, TX: Word Books, 1981.

Schimmels, Cliff. *How to Help Your Child Survive & Thrive in Public School.* Old Tappan, NJ: Fleming H. Revell, 1982.

CHAPTER 8

Landorf, Joyce. *Balcony People.* Waco, TX: Word Books, 1984.

LeFever, Marlene. *Creative Hospitality.* Wheaton, IL: Tyndale House, 1980.

McGinnis, Alan. *The Friendship Factor.* Minneapolis, MN: Augsburg Publishing House, 1979.

York, Phyllis and York, David. *Toughlove.* Doubleday, 1982.

CHAPTER 9

Carroll, Frances Loftiss. *How to Talk With Your Children About God.*

Haystead, Wes. *Teaching Your Child About God.* Ventura, CA: Regal Books, 1981.

Henrichsen, Walter A. *How to Discipline Your Children.* Wheaton, IL: Victor Books, 1981.

Murray, Andrew. *How to Bring Your Children to Christ.* Springdale, PA: Whitaker House, 1984.

Swindoll, Charles R. *You and Your Child.* Nashville, TN: Thomas Nelson, 1977.

Walk Thru the Bible Ministries, Inc. *The Family Walk,* P.O. Box 80587, Atlanta, GA 30366; 1983.

Wilt, Joy. *Happily Ever After.* Waco, TX: Word Books, 1977.

CHAPTER 10

Allen, Ronald and Allen, Beverly. *Liberated Traditionalism.* Portland, OR: Multnomah Press, 1985.

Bennett, Rita. *I'm Glad You Asked That.* Old Tappan, NJ: Fleming H. Revell, 1983.

Burkett, Larry. *Your Finances in Changing Times.* Chicago, IL: Moody Press, 1982.

MacArthur, John Jr. *The Family.* Chicago, IL: Moody Press, 1982.

Yohn, Rick. *God's Answers to Financial Problems.* Eugene, OR: Harvest House, 1978.

CHAPTER 11

Briscoe, Jill. *Queen of Hearts.* Old Tappan, NJ: Fleming H. Revell, 1984.

Dobson, James. *What Wives Wish Their Husbands Knew About Woman.* Wheaton, IL: Tyndale House, 1977.

Gaither, Gloria and Dobson, Shirley. *Let's Make a Memory.* Waco, TX: Word Books, 1983.

MacDonald, Gail. *High Call, High Privilege.* Wheaton, IL: Tyndale House, 1981.

Wallace, Joanne. *The Confident Woman.* Old Tappan, NJ: Fleming H. Revell, 1984.

Yohn, Rick. *Finding Time, A Christian Approach to Life Management.* Waco, TX: Word Books, 1984.